digits™

PEARSON

Boston, Massachusetts • Chandler, Arizona • Glenview, Illinois • Upper Saddle River, New Jersey

Acknowledgments: Illustrations by Ralph Voltz and Laserwords

ISBN-13: 978-0-13-318096-1
ISBN-10: 0-13-318096-4
9 10 11 12   V011   15 14 13 12

digits™ System Requirements

Supported System Configurations

	Operating System (32-bit only)	Web Browser* (32-bit only)	Java™ (JRE) Version**	JavaScript® Version***
PC	Windows® XP (SP3)	Internet Explorer® 7	Version 5.0, Update 11 or higher	1.4.2
	Windows Vista (SP1)	Internet Explorer 8	Version 5.0, Update 11 or higher	1.5
	Windows 7	Internet Explorer 9 (in compatibility mode)	Version 6.0, up to Update 18	1.6
Mac	Macintosh® OS 10.6	Safari® 5.0 and 5.1	Version 5.0, Update 16 or higher	1.5

* Pop-up blockers must be disabled in the browser.
** Java (JRE) plug-in must be installed.
*** JavaScript must be enabled in the browser.

Additional Requirements

Software	Version
Adobe® Flash®	Version 10.1 or higher
Adobe Reader® (required for PC*)	Version 8 or higher
Word processing software	Microsoft® Word®, Open Office, or similar application to open ".doc" files

* Macintosh® OS 10.6 has a built-in PDF reader, Preview.

Screen Resolution
Minimum: 1024 x 768*
Maximum: 1280 x 1024
*recommended for interactive whiteboards

Internet Connection
Broadband (cable/DSL) or greater is recommended.

Firefox® and Chrome™ Users
You cannot use the Firefox or Chrome browsers to log in or view courses.

AOL® and AT&T™ Yahoo!® Users
You cannot use the AOL or AT&T Yahoo! browsers. However, you can use AOL or AT&T as your Internet Service Provider to access the Internet, and then open a supported browser.

For digits™ Support
go to **http://support.pearsonschool.com/index.cfm/digits**

My Name: _____

My Teacher's Name: _____

My School: _____

Lisa

Jay

Andie

Kamal

Francis (Skip) Fennell
digits Author

Approaches to mathematics content and curriculum, educational policy, and support for intervention

Eric Milou
digits Author

Approaches to mathematical content and the use of technology in middle grades classrooms

Art Johnson
digits Author

Approaches to mathematical content and support for English language learners

William F. Tate
digits Author

Approaches to intervention, and use of efficacy and research

Helene Sherman
digits Author

Teacher education and support for struggling students

Grant Wiggins
digits Consulting Author

Understanding by Design

Stuart J. Murphy
digits Author

Visual learning and student engagement

Randall I. Charles
digits Advisor

Janie Schielack
digits Author

Approaches to mathematical content, building problem solvers, and support for intervention

Jim Cummins
digits Advisor

Supporting English Language Learners

Jacquie Moen
digits Advisor

Digital Technology

Log into **MyMathUniverse**

Be sure to save all of your your log-in information by writing it here.

Class URL: _____

My Username: _____

My Password: _____

1 First, go to MyMathUniverse.com.

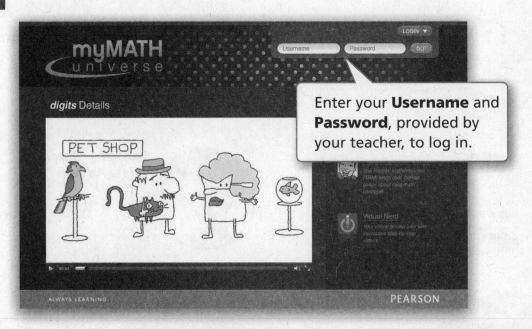

Enter your **Username** and **Password**, provided by your teacher, to log in.

2 After you've logged in, choose your class from the **home page.**

Choose **your class** from the list.

3 When you have chosen your class, this is your **Overview page.**

Click **To Do** to view your due items.

Click **Practice** to explore *digits* lessons on your own.

Click **Done** to view your past due and completed items.

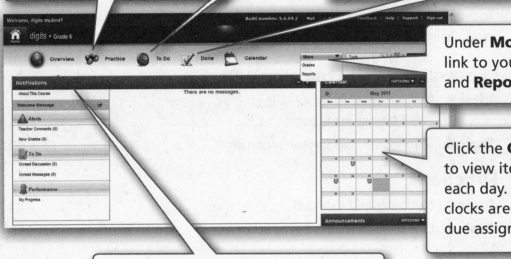

Under **More** you can link to your **Grades** and **Reports**.

Click the **Calendar** to view items due each day. Red alarm clocks are for past due assignments!

Check your **Notifications**, including:
- Teacher Comments
- Grades posted
- Messages from your teacher
- Your progress in *digits*

As you work online, make sure to hit "Save" so you don't lose your work!

Save

Welcome to digits.

Using the Student Companion

digits is designed to help you master mathematics skills and concepts in a way that's relevant to you. As the title **digits** suggests, this program takes a digital approach. The Student Companion supports your work on **digits** by providing a place to demonstrate your understanding of lesson skills and concepts in writing.

Your companion supports your work on **digits** in so many ways!

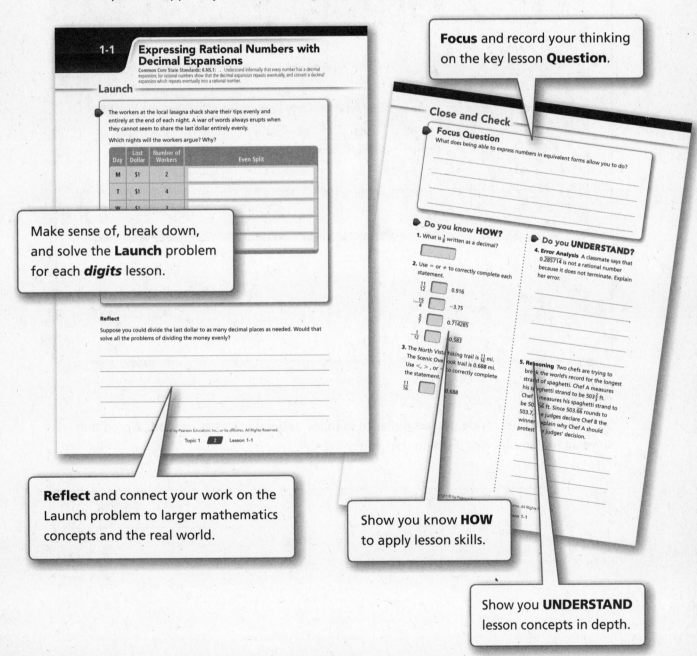

Focus and record your thinking on the key lesson **Question**.

Make sense of, break down, and solve the **Launch** problem for each **digits** lesson.

Reflect and connect your work on the Launch problem to larger mathematics concepts and the real world.

Show you know **HOW** to apply lesson skills.

Show you **UNDERSTAND** lesson concepts in depth.

1-1

Expressing Rational Numbers with Decimal Expansions

Common Core State Standards: 8.NS.1: ... Understand informally that every number has a decimal expansion; for rational numbers show that the decimal expansion repeats eventually, and convert a decimal expansion which repeats eventually into a rational number.

Launch

The workers at the local lasagna shack share their tips evenly and entirely at the end of each night. A war of words always erupts when they cannot seem to share the last dollar entirely evenly.

Which nights will the workers argue? Why?

Day	Last Dollar	Number of Workers	Even Split
M	$1	2	
T	$1	4	
W	$1	3	
TH	$1	5	
F	$1	6	

Reflect

Suppose you could divide the last dollar to as many decimal places as needed. Would that solve all the problems of dividing the money evenly?

_____

_____

_____

_____

Close and Check

Focus Question

What does being able to express numbers in equivalent forms allow you to do?

_____

_____

_____

_____

Do you know HOW?

1. What is $\frac{1}{8}$ written as a decimal?

2. Use $=$ or $\neq$ to correctly complete each statement.

$\frac{11}{12}$ ⬜ 0.916

$-\frac{15}{4}$ ⬜ -3.75

$\frac{5}{7}$ ⬜ $0.\overline{714285}$

$-\frac{1}{12}$ ⬜ $-0.58\overline{3}$

3. The North Vista hiking trail is $\frac{11}{16}$ mi. The Scenic Overlook trail is 0.688 mi. Use $<$, $>$, or $=$ to correctly complete the statement.

$\frac{11}{16}$ ⬜ 0.688

Do you UNDERSTAND?

4. Error Analysis A classmate says that $0.\overline{285714}$ is not a rational number because it does not terminate. Explain her error.

_____

_____

_____

_____

_____

5. Reasoning Two chefs are trying to break the world's record for the longest strand of spaghetti. Chef A measures his spaghetti strand to be $503\frac{2}{3}$ ft. Chef B measures his spaghetti strand to be $503.\overline{66}$ ft. Since $503.\overline{66}$ rounds to 503.7, the judges declare Chef B the winner. Explain why Chef A should protest the judges' decision.

_____

_____

_____

_____

Exploring Irrational Numbers

Common Core State Standards: 8.NS.1: Know that numbers that are not rational are called irrational. Understand informally that every number has a decimal expansion; for rational numbers show that the decimal expansion repeats eventually . . . .

Launch

 Complete the table and then draw each square. Provide exact lengths. Describe any problems you have.

	Side Length	Area
Square 1		1 unit^2
Square 2		2 units^2
Square 3		4 units^2

Square 1		Square 2		Square 3	

Reflect

Do you think you could find an exact side length for all of the squares if you kept trying? Explain.

_____

_____

_____

_____

Close and Check

Focus Question

What is the difference between an irrational number and a rational number? Can a number be both irrational and rational?

_____

_____

_____

_____

Do you know HOW?

1. Circle the irrational numbers.

$\sqrt{111}$ $\sqrt{400}$ $\sqrt{160}$

$\sqrt{144}$ $\sqrt{220}$ $\sqrt{200}$

2. Circle the rational numbers. Assume each pattern continues.

4.014014   6.232342345

0.717717   1.594593592

12.12211222   9.96939693

3. Indicate all the possible names for each number.

	$\sqrt{36}$	$-\frac{1}{6}$	$\sqrt{11}$
Natural Number			
Whole Number			
Integer			
Rational Number			
Irrational Number			
Real Number			

Do you UNDERSTAND?

4. Reasoning Can an irrational number ever be a natural number? A whole number? Explain.

_____

_____

_____

_____

_____

5. Compare and Contrast What is the difference between locating $\frac{3}{5}$ on a number line and locating $\sqrt{5}$ on a number line?

_____

_____

_____

_____

Approximating Irrational Numbers

Common Core State Standards: 8.NS.2: Use rational approximations of irrational numbers to compare the size of irrational numbers, locate them approximately on a number line diagram, and estimate the value of expressions.

Launch

Due to the sauciness of their sauce, the local lasagna shack decides to expand its old square napkin to a new square napkin.

Find the approximate side length of the new square napkin. Explain what you did.

Old Napkin
100 in.²

New Napkin
150 in.²

Reflect

Why would it be useful to write the side length of the new square napkin as an approximate length instead of an exact length?

_____

_____

_____

_____

Close and Check

Focus Question

How do you estimate an irrational number? Why might you need to be able to estimate an irrational number?

_____

_____

_____

_____

Do you know HOW?

1. On a number line, between which two whole numbers would $\sqrt{136}$ be located?

[ ] and [ ]

2. The square root of an integer n is between 6 and 7. Write an inequality that expresses all the possible values for n.

[ ]

3. Which value is farther to the right on a number line?

2.5^2 $\sqrt{81}$

[ ]

4. A square sandbox has an area of 42 ft². What is the approximate perimeter of the sandbox to the nearest hundredth?

[ ]

Do you UNDERSTAND?

5. Reasoning Two classmates estimate the location of $\sqrt{60}$ on a number line. One student locates the point at 7.7. The other student says the point is located at 7.75. Can both students be correct? Explain.

_____

_____

_____

_____

6. Writing Pi (π) is an irrational number used to find the circumference and area of circles. Are the circumference and area of a circle actual or estimated measures? Explain.

_____

_____

_____

_____

_____

Comparing and Ordering Rational and Irrational Numbers

Common Core State Standards: 8.NS.2: Use rational approximations of irrational numbers to compare the size of irrational numbers, locate them approximately on a number line diagram, and estimate the value of expressions.

Launch

For people who prefer pizza, the local lasagna shack also offers thin crust pizzas in three different shapes. Each costs $20.

Which deal is the best and which deal is the worst? Explain.

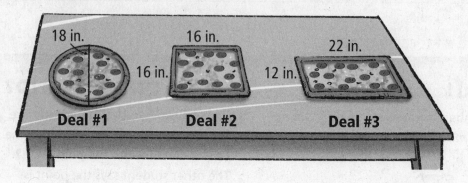

Reflect

Do you think all the pizza areas are rational? Explain.

_____

_____

_____

Close and Check

Focus Question

How can you compare rational and irrational numbers? Why might you want to?

_____

_____

_____

_____

Do you know HOW?

1. Use $<$, $>$, or $=$ to complete each statement.

7 ⬚ $\sqrt{7}$

$\sqrt{121}$ ⬚ 11

-16 ⬚ $-\sqrt{225}$

$\sqrt{8}$ ⬚ $\dfrac{21}{8}$

2. Order the values from least to greatest

$\dfrac{25}{7}$ $\sqrt{3}$ 5.85 4^2 π

3. Match each point on the number line to the nearest value.

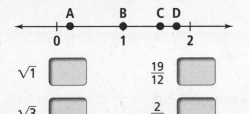

$\sqrt{1}$ ⬚ $\dfrac{19}{12}$ ⬚

$\sqrt{3}$ ⬚ $\dfrac{2}{11}$ ⬚

Do you UNDERSTAND?

4. Reasoning The owners want to remake the pizza in Deal #3 of the Launch. Can they make a square pizza with exactly the same area? Explain.

_____

_____

_____

_____

_____

5. Writing What strategies can you use to order the numbers in Exercise 2 without changing them all to decimals?

_____

_____

_____

_____

_____

_____

Problem Solving

Common Core State Standards: 8.NS.1: Know that numbers that are not rational are called irrational … and convert a decimal expansion which repeats eventually into a rational number. **8.NS.2:** Use rational approximations of irrational numbers to … estimate the value of expressions.

Launch

Your friend said the square root of 14 is somewhere in between 3 and 4 as shown.

Explain whether you agree. Then show where would be a more precise spot to place the square root of 14 and tell why your estimate is better.

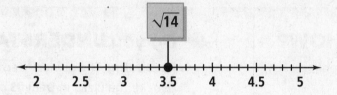

Reflect

When is precision important and when is it not so important? Provide an example for each.

_____

_____

_____

_____

Close and Check

Focus Question

How is solving a problem that includes rational numbers similar to solving a problem that includes irrational numbers? How is it different?

_____

_____

_____

_____

Do you know HOW?

1. If $x = 6$, what is the smallest natural number y that makes $\sqrt{x^2 + y^2}$ rational?

$y = $ ▢

2. A carnival ride must be enclosed within a fence. The ride requires 676 ft² of space to operate. What is the minimum number of feet of fencing required to enclose the ride?

▢ ft

3. A square billboard is shown below. What is the approximate length and width of the billboard to the nearest hundredth?

$A = 5,200$ ft²

▢

Do you UNDERSTAND?

4. Reasoning A square pool with side lengths of 16 ft sells for $\frac{2}{3}$ the price of a circular pool with a diameter of 18 ft. If the shape does not matter, which is the better deal? Explain.

_____

_____

_____

_____

5. Error Analysis Your friend says that 0.2 and $0.\overline{2}$ can both be written as the fraction $\frac{1}{5}$. Explain his mistake.

_____

_____

_____

_____

Solving Two-Step Equations

Common Core State Standard: 8.EE.7: Solve linear equations in one variable. 8.EE.7.b: Solve linear equations with rational number coefficients, including equations whose solutions require expanding expressions using the distributive property and collecting like terms.

Launch

Two friends shovel snow on a winter Saturday. Some people pay them their fee by handing them cash. Some give them their fee in an envelope. They split the money they make evenly.

What is their shoveling fee? Explain how you know.

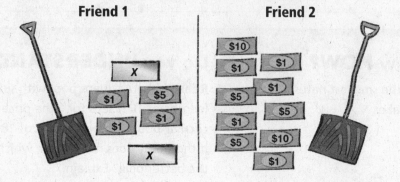

Reflect

Could you write an equation for this problem? How might that help?

_____

_____

_____

_____

Close and Check

Focus Question

What kinds of problems need two operations?

_____

_____

_____

_____

Do you know HOW?

1. Solve for x.

$$63 = 12x - 9$$

$x = \boxed{}$

2. A cell phone plan includes a monthly rate of $19.95 plus $0.55 per minute for international calls. The bill is $95.30. Write and solve an equation to determine how many minutes were spent on international calls.

[   ]

3. A family buys 132 ft^2 of carpet for the guest bedroom and 270 ft^2 of carpet for the family room. They spend $1,201.98 on new carpet. What is the average cost per square foot for the new carpeting?

Do you UNDERSTAND?

4. Reasoning Which operation did you use first to solve Exercise 1? Explain.

_____

_____

_____

_____

_____

5. Error Analysis A classmate solves the equation shown. Explain his error and tell how you would solve it.

$$1.25x + 7.4 = 10.4$$
$$100(1.25x) + 10(7.4) = 10(10.4)$$
$$125x + 74 = 104$$
$$125x = 30$$
$$x = 0.24$$

_____

_____

_____

_____

Solving Equations with Variables on Both Sides

Common Core State Standard: 8.EE.7: Solve linear equations in one variable. **8.EE.7.b:** Solve linear equations with rational number coefficients, including equations whose solutions require expanding expressions using the distributive property and collecting like terms.

Launch

Two friends mow lawns on a spring Saturday. Some people pay them their fee by handing them cash. Some people give them their fee in an envelope. They split the money they make evenly.

What is their lawn-mowing fee? Explain how you know.

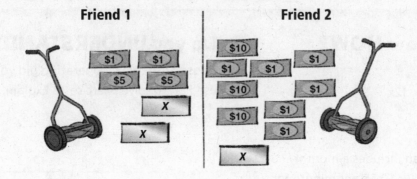

Reflect

In the snow-shoveling problem in Lesson 2-1, only one friend had an envelope. The other friend had all cash. Was this problem more difficult because both friends had envelopes? Explain.

_____

_____

_____

_____

Close and Check

Focus Question

Why do some equations have the same variable on both sides?

_____

_____

_____

_____

Do you know HOW?

1. What is the value of x when the expression $3x + 6$ equals the expression $-15 + 6x$?

$x = $ ☐

2. Two friends race. The first friend gets a head start and runs at a steady rate of 0.20 miles per minute. The second friend waits 1 minute and then runs at a steady rate of 0.25 miles per minute. How long will it take for the second runner to catch up with the first?

☐

3. Solve $72x + 436 = -96x + 1108$.

☐

4. You have $12.50 in a savings account. You deposit $7.25 more each week. Your friend has $32.50 in a savings account. She deposits $5.25 more each week. In how many weeks will the amount of money in the accounts be equal?

☐ weeks

Do you UNDERSTAND?

5. Reasoning If the two friends in Exercise 2 race for 4 miles at their constant rates, who will win the race? Explain.

_____

_____

_____

_____

6. Compare and Contrast How is solving an equation with the variable on both sides of the equation the same as and different from solving an equation with the variable on one side of the equation?

_____

_____

_____

_____

_____

Solving Equations Using the Distributive Property

Common Core State Standard: 8.EE.7b: Solve linear equations with rational number coefficients, including equations whose solutions require expanding expressions using the distributive property and collecting like terms.

Launch

Match the equivalent expressions. Tell how you know your matches are correct.

| $-3(-s + 5)$ | $3s - 15$ | $3(-s + 5)$ |

| $-3(s - 5)$ | $-3s + 15$ | $3(s - 5)$ |

Reflect

Which expressions were the simplest to match? Which were the hardest to match? Explain.

_____

_____

_____

_____

_____

Close and Check

Focus Question

How can you model a problem with an equation that uses the Distributive Property?

_____

_____

_____

_____

Do you know HOW?

1. Use the Distributive Property to solve
$3(11r - 13) = -7r + 57 + 32r$.

2. Circle the correct solution to the
equation $\frac{7}{9}x - 6 = 17$.

A. $\frac{9}{7}\left(\frac{7}{9}x\right) - 6 = \frac{9}{7}(17)$

$x - 6 = \frac{153}{7}$

$x = \frac{153}{7} + \frac{42}{7}$

$x = \frac{195}{7}$

B. $\frac{7}{9}x = 17 + 6$

$\frac{9}{7}\left(\frac{7}{9}x\right) = \frac{9}{7}(23)$

$x = \frac{207}{7}$

3. The width of a rectangle is 17 yd
shorter than the length. The perimeter
of the rectangle is 126 yd. Find the
width of the rectangle.

Do you UNDERSTAND?

4. Error Analysis Explain the error made
in the incorrect solution in Exercise 2.

_____

_____

_____

_____

_____

5. Reasoning Write an equation for the
perimeter of the rectangle in Exercise 3
in terms of the length ℓ. How is this
equation different than an equation
for the perimeter in terms of the
width w?

_____

_____

_____

_____

_____

_____

Solutions – One, None, or Infinitely Many

Common Core State Standard: 8.EE.7: Solve linear equations in one variable. **8.EE.7.a:** Give examples of linear equations … with one solution, infinitely many solutions, or no solutions. Show which … is the case by successively transforming the given equation into simpler forms … .

Launch

Evaluate each expression using different values for *s*. Then, tell what you know about the expressions.

s	3(4s + 8)	2(12 + 6s)

Reflect

Could you have reached the same conclusion about the expressions without trying different values for *s*? Explain.

_____

_____

_____

_____

_____

Close and Check

Focus Question

What does it mean if an equation is simplified to $0 = 0$? Do all problems have exactly one solution?

_____

_____

_____

_____

Do you know HOW?

1. Write *none, one,* or *many* to identify the number of solutions to each equation.

$\frac{2}{3}x + 15 = \frac{4}{6}x + 15$

$6 = 3^2$

$2.7y - 9 = 18$

2. Solve $5(12 - d) + d = 2d - 6$.

3. Solve $7t - (t + 5) = 6t + 5$.

4. Solve $\frac{2}{3}\left(9s - \frac{3}{2}\right) = s(0.45 + 5) + 1.2$.

Do you UNDERSTAND?

5. **Writing** Explain how to identify whether an equation has no solution, one solution, or infinitely many solutions.

_____

_____

_____

_____

_____

6. **Error Analysis** A classmate solves the equation $8 + 2(8r - 2r) = 4(3r + 2)$. She says $r = 0$ is the only solution. Is she correct? Explain.

_____

_____

_____

_____

_____

Problem Solving

Common Core State Standard: 8.EE.7: Solve linear equations in one variable. **8.EE.7.a:** Give examples of linear equations in one variable with one solution, infinitely many solutions, or no solutions ... .

Launch

Two friends argue over how much to bill for a two-hour raking job. They charge their normal hourly rate plus $2.75 for lawn bags.

Write and solve equations to show how each friend could be correct. Then tell who you think is right and why.

Let's charge $36.

They only owe us $33.25.

Friend 1   **Friend 2**

Reflect

How did the money problem context affect the solution to this problem? Explain.

_____

_____

_____

_____

Close and Check

Focus Question

If you can describe a situation in two different ways, how do you use that information to solve a problem?

_____

_____

_____

_____

Do you know HOW?

1. A delivery driver earns $7.50 per hour and $2 per delivery. Each week, the driver spends $28 on vehicle maintenance and $86 on gas. If the driver works 40 hours per week, how many deliveries are needed each week to earn $300 a week after expenses?

☐ deliveries

2. The total cost, after additional fees, for three tickets to the dinner theater is $322.92. The fees include a 2% service charge and a 15% gratuity. What is the cost of one dinner theater ticket before the fees are added?

☐

3. Craft club members pay $39 a year plus $9 for each craft kit. Non-members can buy craft kits for $12 each. How many kits will have to be bought for the price of membership and non-membership to be equal?

☐ kits

Do you UNDERSTAND?

4. Writing Two students solve the equation. Can both students be correct? Explain.

$$5(3r - 6) = 10r - 10$$

Student A	Student B
$15r - 30 = 10r - 10$	$3r - 6 = 2r - 2$
$5r = 20$	$r = 4$
$r = 4$	

_____

_____

_____

_____

_____

5. Reasoning Would Student B's method work if the equation were $5(3r - 6) = 11r - 14$? Explain.

_____

_____

_____

_____

Perfect Squares, Square Roots, and Equations of the Form $x^2 = p$

Common Core State Standards: 8.EE.2: Use square root and cube root symbols to represent solutions to equations of the form $x^2 = p$ and $x^3 = p$, where p is a positive rational number. Evaluate square roots of small perfect squares and cube roots of small perfect cubes.

Launch

Your friend claims that x^2 is the same as $2x$. Tell how he could have come to that conclusion. Explain whether you agree.

They're the same, right?

x^2 $2x$

Reflect

When have you used expressions with exponents like x^2 in mathematics before? Explain.

_____

_____

_____

_____

Close and Check

Focus Question

How can you apply what you know about squares and square roots to write and solve equations of the form $x^2 = p$? How can you use equations in that form?

_____

_____

_____

_____

Do you know HOW?

1. Solve each equation.

   A. $x^2 = 36$

   B. $x^2 = 64$

   C. $x^2 = 400$

   D. $x^2 = 121$

2. Solve $y^2 = \frac{144}{169}$.

3. A square flower garden has an area of 136 ft². Find the length of one side of the garden to the nearest tenth of a foot.

    ft

4. A square playground has an area of 1,500 ft². Find the length of one side of the playground to the nearest tenth of a foot.

    ft

Do you UNDERSTAND?

5. **Vocabulary** What is the relationship between perfect squares and square roots? Give an example.

   _____

   _____

   _____

   _____

6. **Error Analysis** The square-shaped downtown region of a town has an area of 144 km². Your friend says the length of one side can be represented by $\sqrt{144} = \pm 12$. Explain the error she made in her solution.

   _____

   _____

   _____

   _____

   _____

Perfect Cubes, Cube Roots, and Equations of the Form $x^3 = p$

Common Core State Standards: 8.EE.2: Use square root and cube root symbols to represent solutions to equations of the form $x^2 = p$ and $x^3 = p$, where p is a positive rational number. Evaluate square roots of small perfect squares and cube roots of small perfect cubes.

Launch

Draw a line from each measurement to the figure it could represent.
Explain how you know you are correct.

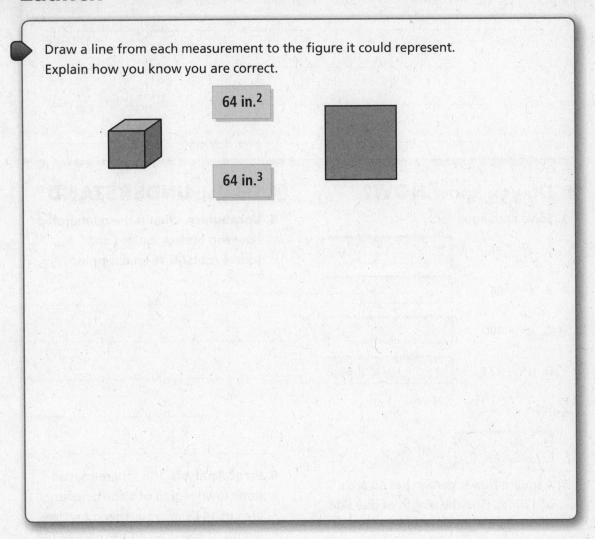

64 in.²

64 in.³

Reflect

Could one of the measurements somehow represent something about both figures?
Could the other?

_____

_____

_____

_____

Close and Check

Focus Question

How is solving an equation that includes cubes similar to solving an equation that includes squares? How is it different?

_____

_____

_____

_____

Do you know HOW?

1. Solve each equation.

A. $x^3 = 343$

B. $x^3 = -1,000$

C. $x^3 = -729$

D. $x^3 = 216$

2. Solve $y^3 = \frac{27}{512}$.

3. A storage unit in the shape of a cube has a volume of 3,000 cubic feet. Find the length of one side of the storage unit to the nearest tenth of a foot.

 ft

4. An abstract sculpture in the shape of a cube has a volume of 925 ft³. Find the approximate length of one side of the sculpture to the nearest tenth of a foot.

 ft

Do you UNDERSTAND?

5. Error Analysis A salesperson says the volume of a cube-shaped birdcage is 64 ft³. What error does the salesperson make when solving the equation? Write the correct solution and explain what it means.

$$x^3 = 64$$
$$\sqrt[3]{x^3} = \sqrt[3]{64}$$
$$x = \pm 4$$

_____

_____

_____

_____

6. Reasoning Can the cube root of a positive number ever be negative? Explain.

_____

_____

_____

_____

3-3

Exponents and Multiplication

Common Core State Standards: 8.EE.1: Know and apply the properties of integer exponents to generate equivalent numerical expressions. *For example, $3^2 \times 3^{-5} = 3^{-3} = \frac{1}{3^3} = \frac{1}{27}$.*

Launch

The city's second-best scientist's first rocket fails to reach orbit. He promises his second rocket will fly twice as fast as his first and his third rocket will fly twice as fast as the second.

How fast will Rockets 2 and 3 fly? Show how you know.

Rocket 1

2^{14} mph

Rocket 2

Rocket 3

Reflect

What do you know about the factors in the expression 2^{14}? Explain.

_____

_____

_____

_____

Close and Check

Focus Question

How can you apply what you know about multiplying numerical expressions to multiplying algebraic expressions containing exponents?

_____

_____

_____

_____

Do you know HOW?

1. Simplify the expression.
$4x^6 \cdot 12x^9$

2. Simplify the expression.
$(f^8)^3$

3. Simplify the expression.
$(4st)^4$

4. Simplify the expression.
$(7q^7r^3)^3$

5. Circle the expression(s) that is equivalent to $216a^9b^{15}c^{27}$.

A. $(72a^6b^{12}c^{24})^3$

B. $(72a^3b^5c^9)^3$

C. $(6a^6b^{12}c^{24})^3$

D. $(6a^3b^5c^9)^3$

Do you UNDERSTAND?

6. Writing Use arithmetic to prove it is incorrect to add the exponents of unlike bases. Use the equation $a^2b^2 \neq (ab)^4$.

_____

_____

_____

_____

7. Error Analysis A classmate says $3s^4 \cdot 5s^2 = (15s)^6$. Explain why your classmate is incorrect. Rewrite the equation to make a true statement.

_____

_____

_____

_____

_____

_____

_____

3-4   **Exponents and Division**

Common Core State Standards: 8.EE.1: Know and apply the properties of integer exponents to generate equivalent numerical expressions. *For example,* $3^2 \times 3^{-5} = 3^{-3} = \frac{1}{3^3} = \frac{1}{27}.$

Launch

The city's second-best scientist likes to look overly complex. That's why he's second best. He presents the cost of a rocket bolt on Rocket 1 as shown.

How much does a bolt really cost? Show how you know.

 $$\frac{5 \cdot 6 \cdot 2 \cdot 17 \cdot 31 \cdot 4 \cdot 4}{31 \cdot 4 \cdot 2 \cdot 17 \cdot 6 \cdot 5}$$ **dollars each**

Reflect

What was the key to solving this problem? Explain.

_____

_____

_____

_____

Close and Check

Focus Question

How can you apply what you know about dividing numerical expressions to dividing algebraic expressions containing exponents?

_____

_____

_____

_____

Do you know HOW?

1. Simplify the expression.

$$\frac{x^{27}}{x^{13}}$$

2. Simplify the expression.

$$\frac{r^{55}}{r^{32}}$$

3. Simplify the expression.

$$\left(\frac{2r^9}{3m}\right)^3$$

4. Simplify the expression.

$$\left(\frac{2d^3g^{12}}{4s^{12}w^6}\right)^5$$

Do you UNDERSTAND?

5. Writing Can the exponent in the denominator be subtracted from the exponent in the numerator when the bases are different? Explain.

_____

_____

_____

_____

6. Error Analysis When asked to simplify the expression, your classmate writes the following:

$$\left(\frac{c^3}{3d^5}\right)^2 = \frac{2c^5}{6d^7}$$

What errors did your classmate make? What should she have written?

_____

_____

_____

_____

Zero and Negative Exponents

Common Core State Standards: 8.EE.1: Know and apply the properties of integer exponents to generate equivalent numerical expressions. *For example,* $3^2 \times 3^{-5} = 3^{-3} = \frac{1}{3^3} = \frac{1}{27}$.

Launch

 Complete the table. Describe three patterns you see in the table.

2^x	10^x
$2^5 = 32$	$10^5 = 100{,}000$
$2^4 = 16$	$10^4 = 10{,}000$
$2^3 = 8$	$10^3 = 1{,}000$
$2^2 = 4$	$10^2 = 100$
$2^1 = $	$10^1 = $
$2^0 = $	$10^0 = $
$2^{-1} = $	$10^{-1} = $

Reflect

Did you figure out the pattern in the left or right column first? Explain.

_____

_____

_____

_____

Close and Check

Focus Question

When do you need an exponent that is equal to zero? When do you need an exponent that is negative? What makes these exponents useful?

_____

_____

_____

Do you know HOW?

1. Simplify the expression.

$$\frac{n^{15}}{n^{15}}$$

2. Simplify the expression.

$$\frac{12k^{15}}{3k^{18}}$$

3. Tell whether each expression is > 1, < 1, or = 1.

5^{-3}

100^{0}

25^{-2}

7^{2}

Do you UNDERSTAND?

4. Reasoning In the expression $\frac{a^3}{a^3}$, why can the variable *not* be equal to 0? Use substitution to justify your argument arithmetically.

_____

_____

_____

_____

5. Error Analysis Your classmate simplified the expression below. Explain his error and write the correct simplified expression.

$$\frac{6w^{12}}{3w^{12}} = 2w^0 = 2 \cdot 0 = 0$$

_____

_____

_____

_____

Comparing Expressions with Exponents

Common Core State Standards: 8.EE.1: Know and apply the properties of integer exponents to generate equivalent numerical expressions. *For example, $3^2 \times 3^{-5} = 3^{-3} = \frac{1}{3^3} = \frac{1}{27}$.*

Launch

Use the tiles to create an expression with the least value and an expression with the greatest value. For each expression, you must use each number tile and the negative sign tile in only one location.

Tell how you decided the tile locations.

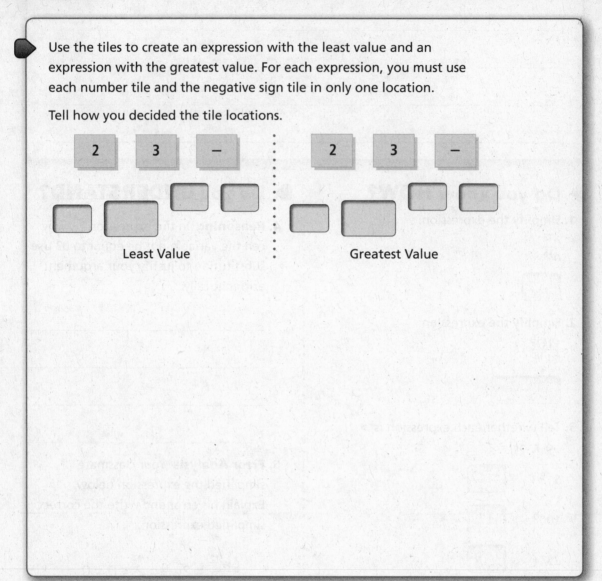

Reflect

What did you decide first in solving the problem? Explain.

_____

_____

_____

_____

Close and Check

Focus Question

What does being able to write expressions with exponents in equivalent forms allow you to do?

_____

_____

_____

_____

Do you know HOW?

1. Which expression(s) is equivalent to 6^{12}?

I. $2^{10} \cdot 3^2$

II. $6^0 \cdot 6^{12}$

III. $(6^{10})^2$

IV. $(6^2)^6$

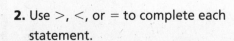

2. Use $>$, $<$, or $=$ to complete each statement.

8^0 ☐ $\dfrac{8^3}{1^3}$

12^6 ☐ $(12^2)^3$

25^8 ☐ 125^5

27^{12} ☐ $(9^6)^3$

$(8^6)^6$ ☐ $(4^4 \cdot 2^2)^6$

Do you UNDERSTAND?

3. Compare and Contrast What is the difference between comparing exponential numbers with like bases and comparing those with unlike bases?

_____

_____

_____

_____

_____

4. Error Analysis A classmate writes equivalent expressions. Her work is shown below. Is she correct? Explain.

$$(4^2 \cdot 3^2)^6 = (12^4)^6 = 12^{24}$$

_____

_____

_____

_____

Problem Solving

Common Core State Standards: 8.EE.1: Know and apply the properties of integer exponents to generate equivalent numerical expressions. *For example,* $3^2 \times 3^{-5} = 3^{-3} = \frac{1}{3^3} = \frac{1}{27}$.

Launch

 Look for a pattern in the table.

Based on the pattern, what value of x makes the statement $4^{15} = 2^x$ true?

Powers of 4	Powers of 2
$4^2 = 16$	$2^4 = 16$
$4^3 = 64$	$2^6 = 64$
$4^4 = 256$	$2^8 = 256$
$4^5 = 1024$	$2^{10} = 1024$

Reflect

What property of exponents did you apply to help you solve this problem?

_____

_____

Did you use an equation to find the value of x? If so, what equation did you use?

_____

_____

_____

Close and Check

Focus Question
What kind of problems can you solve using expressions and equations containing exponents?

_____

_____

_____

_____

Do you know HOW?

1. Circle the value(s) of s for which the expression $-9s^3$ is reasonable for representing the volume of a cube.

   A. $s = 0$

   B. s can be any negative number.

   C. s can be any positive number.

2. Circle the value(s) of y for which the expression $35y^2$ is reasonable for representing the number of square yards your friend mows.

   A. $y = 0$

   B. y can be any negative number.

   C. y can be any positive number.

3. For what values of d, if any, will $2d^4 = 1{,}250$?

   [   ]

Do you UNDERSTAND?

4. **Reasoning** How would the solution to Exercise 3 change if the equation was $2d^4 = -1{,}250$? How do you know?

   _____

   _____

   _____

   _____

   _____

5. **Error Analysis** Your friend writes an expression to represent the score of a game. Is his expression useful? Explain.

$$\frac{5p^6}{(p^2)^3}$$

   _____

   _____

   _____

   _____

Exploring Scientific Notation

Common Core State Standards: 8.EE.3: Use numbers expressed in the form of a single digit times an integer power of 10 to estimate very large or very small quantities … . **8.EE.4:** Perform operations with numbers expressed in scientific notation … .

Launch

Order the tiles from least to greatest numeric value.
Explain how you know your order is correct.

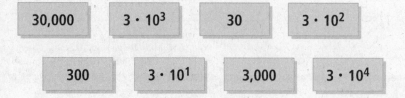

| 30,000 | $3 \cdot 10^3$ | 30 | $3 \cdot 10^2$ |

| 300 | $3 \cdot 10^1$ | 3,000 | $3 \cdot 10^4$ |

Reflect

Is there a pattern between the numbers and the expressions? If so, describe it.

_____

_____

_____

_____

Close and Check

Focus Question
Why might you use powers of 10 to write numbers?

_____

_____

_____

_____

▶ Do you know **HOW?**

1. Order the numbers from least to greatest.

Least

7.29×10^0 [ ]

7.29×10^{-5} [ ]

7.29×10^3 [ ]

7.29×10^{-3} [ ]

Greatest

2. Circle the numbers that are expressed in scientific notation.

34.5×10^7 5.02×10^3

2×10^9 0.4×10^1

3. Suppose your calculator display shows 6.5E+21. Express this result in scientific notation.

[ ]

4. Write 745,000 in scientific notation.

[ ]

▶ Do you **UNDERSTAND?**

5. Reasoning Explain the strategy you used to order the numbers in Exercise 1.

_____

_____

_____

_____

_____

_____

6. Vocabulary How is scientific notation useful in mathematics?

_____

_____

_____

_____

_____

Using Scientific Notation to Describe Very Large Quantities

Common Core State Standards: 8.EE.3: Use numbers expressed in the form of a single digit times an integer power of 10 to estimate very large or very small quantities, and to express how many times as much one is than the other … .

Launch

Your friend writes 5×2^6 as a shortcut for writing 1×10^6. Explain your friend's shortcut thinking. Is your friend's thinking more science or fiction?

Shorter is always better!

1×10^6

5×2^6

Reflect

Why is it helpful to write numbers in scientific notation using powers of 10? Why is this better than using powers of 2? Explain.

_____

_____

_____

_____

Close and Check

Focus Question

How can positive powers of 10 make large numbers easier to write and compare?

_____

_____

_____

_____

_____

Do you know HOW?

1. The X-15 aircraft holds the world speed record at 23,865,600 ft/hr. Express the world record speed in scientific notation.

2. The population on Earth increased by about 7.62×10^8 people during the first decade of the 21st century. Express the population growth in standard form.

  people

3. One giant ant colony is reported to have about 3.06×10^8 worker ants and 1.02×10^6 queen ants. The number of worker ants is how many times the number of queen ants?

Do you UNDERSTAND?

4. Writing Your best friend has never learned about scientific notation. Explain how to use scientific notation to rewrite very large numbers.

_____

_____

_____

_____

_____

_____

5. Error Analysis A friend says the average distance to the moon is 382,500 km. Is the number he wrote accurate? Explain.

$$3.825 \times 10^6$$

_____

_____

Copyright © by Pearson Education, Inc., or its affiliates. All Rights Reserved.

Topic 4   39   Lesson 4-2

Using Scientific Notation to Describe Very Small Quantities

Common Core State Standards: 8.EE.3: Use numbers expressed in the form of a single digit times an integer power of 10 to estimate very large or very small quantities, and to express how many times as much one is than the other ... .

Launch

 Your friend says a zeptometer is 1×10^{-21} based on its standard form. Explain your friend's zepto-reasoning. Is your friend's thinking more science or fiction?

Unit	Scientific Notation (m)	Standard Form (m)
Meter	1×10^{0}	1
Decimeter	1×10^{-1}	0.1
Centimeter	1×10^{-2}	0.01
Millimeter	1×10^{-3}	0.001
Zeptometer		0.000000000000000000001

Reflect

Does it make more sense to use scientific notation or standard form to represent 1 zeptometer?

_____

_____

Close and Check

Do you know HOW?

1. The diameter of an average snowflake is about 10 micrometers. That is approximately 0.0003937 in. Express the diameter of a snowflake in scientific notation.

    [   ]

2. The diameters of atoms can vary. One particular atom has a diameter of 5.0×10^{-8} cm. Express the diameter of the atom in standard form.

    [   ]

3. The measurement 8.16 micrometers equals 8.16×10^{-6} meter. The measurement 2.04 centimeters equals 2.04×10^{-2} meter. How many times greater is the centimeter measurement than the micrometer measurement?

    [   ]

Do you UNDERSTAND?

4. **Writing** Do you agree or disagree with the statement below? Explain.

    > Scientific notation is a method used to rewrite very large or very small numbers as a number n greater than 0 times an integer power of 10.

    _____

    _____

    _____

5. **Error Analysis** An earthworm travels 0.0000425 miles per second. A friend writes the rate as 4.25×10^5 mps. Explain her error. Write the correct rate in scientific notation.

    _____

    _____

    _____

Operating with Numbers Expressed in Scientific Notation

Common Core State Standards: 8.EE.3: Use numbers expressed in the form of a single digit times an integer power of 10 ... . **8.EE.4:** Perform operations with numbers expressed in scientific notation, including problems where both decimal and scientific notation are used.

Launch

The scientific notation cards shown represent place values. Arrange at least six of the cards in place-value order to represent a three-digit number.

Then write your number in standard form and explain why the cards you chose represent your number.

1×10^2 1×10^2 1×10^0 1×10^1 1×10^1

1×10^1 1×10^0 1×10^2 1×10^2 1×10^2

Reflect

How is using the cards the same as using place value blocks? How is it different?

_____

_____

_____

_____

Close and Check

Focus Question

You previously learned how to multiply and divide expressions with exponents. How can you apply what you know to operations with numbers in scientific notation?

_____

_____

_____

_____

Do you know HOW?

1. Simplify.

$(6.9 \times 10^{12}) - (2.6 \times 10^{12}) + (3.4 \times 10^{12})$

[ ]

2. One gram of dust can contain 2.5×10^5 dust mite droppings. The average six-room home collects about 1.5×10^3 grams of dust each month. In scientific notation, how many dust mite droppings can be found in an average home each month?

[ ] droppings

3. The smallest ant is about 4.9×10^{-4} m in length. The distance around the earth at the equator is about 4×10^7 m. In scientific notation to the nearest tenth, how many of these small ants would it take to circle the earth at the equator?

[ ] ants

Do you UNDERSTAND?

4. Compare and Contrast How are the processes for multiplying and dividing numbers written in scientific notation alike and different?

_____

_____

_____

_____

5. Error Analysis Your friend says this problem has no solution because 8.3 cannot be subtracted from 2.5. Do you argee? Explain.

> Statistically, 2.5×10^7 plastic beverage bottles are used each day. If 8.3×10^6 bottles are recycled, how many end up in landfills?

_____

_____

_____

Problem Solving

Common Core State Standards: 8.EE.4: Perform operations with numbers expressed in scientific notation .... Use scientific notation and choose units of appropriate size for measurements of very large or very small quantities .... Also, **8.EE.1**, **8.EE.3**.

Launch

Approximate population data for adults and children in the most and least populous U.S. states in one year, according to the U.S. Census Bureau, are shown.

What is the total population for each state in scientific notation? Justify your answers.

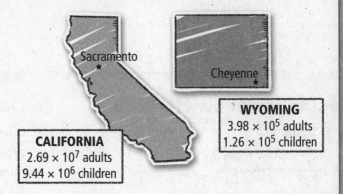

WYOMING
3.98×10^5 adults
1.26×10^5 children

CALIFORNIA
2.69×10^7 adults
9.44×10^6 children

Reflect

How can you tell that California has more people than Wyoming just by comparing the adult and children populations?

_____

_____

_____

_____

Close and Check

> ## Focus Question
> How can you use scientific notation to help you solve problems?
>
> _____
>
> _____
>
> _____

Do you know HOW?

1. It takes light 8.5 minutes to travel from the sun to the earth. Light travels at 9.82×10^8 feet per second. How far does light travel from the sun to the earth? Express this distance in scientific notation using the most appropriate unit from the given list.

$$5280 \text{ ft} = 1760 \text{ yd}$$
$$1760 \text{ yd} = 1 \text{ mi}$$

2. The area of the world's largest country is about 6.6×10^6 mi^2. The area of the world's smallest country is about 1.7×10^{-1} mi^2. About how many times larger is the area of the largest country than the area of the smallest country? Express your answer in scientific notation.

3. Find the value of n.
$$1.887 \times 10^{12} = (5.1 \times 10^8)(3.7 \times 10^n)$$

4. Find the value of n.
$$(4.5 \times 10^9) \div (9 \times 10^n) = 5 \times 10^2$$

Do you UNDERSTAND?

5. **Reasoning** Explain why you chose the unit of measure that you did in Exercise 1. Explain why you did not choose the others.

6. **Compare and Contrast** How can understanding operations on exponential numbers help you solve problems involving scientific notation?

Graphing Proportional Relationships

Common Core State Standards: 8.EE.5: Graph proportional relationships, interpreting the unit rate as the slope of the graph. Compare two different proportional relationships represented in different ways.

Launch

Make a graph based on the data in the table. Give the graph a title and label the axes so it's clear what the variables could represent.

Independent Variable	Dependent Variable
0	0
1	4
2	8
3	12
8	32

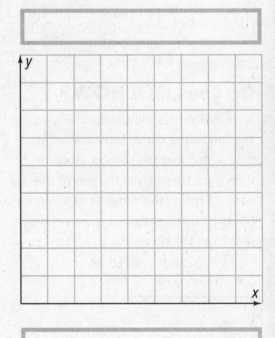

Reflect

Does the table represent a proportional relationship? Explain.

_____

_____

_____

_____

Close and Check

Do you know HOW?

1. You earn $4 in Bonus Bucks for each $50 you spend. Complete the graph to model this situation.

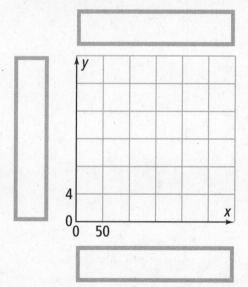

2. A scuba diver descends into the ocean from the surface at a rate of 65 feet per minute. Complete the table of the diver's position relative to the surface.

$$d = -65m$$

Minutes (m)	0	1	2
Depth (d)			

Do you UNDERSTAND?

3. Writing Based on the graph in Exercise 1, is the relationship between the amount spent and the amount of bonus bucks earned proportional? Explain.

4. Reasoning If the diver in Exercise 2 jumped off a boat into the ocean rather than descending from the surface of the ocean, would the relationship still be proportional?

Linear Equations: $y = mx$

Common Core State Standards: 8.EE.5: Graph proportional relationships, interpreting the unit rate as the slope of the graph. Compare two different proportional relationships represented in different ways. **8.EE.6:** ... derive the equation $y = mx$ for a line through the origin ... .

Launch

How are the lines similar? How are they different? Explain.

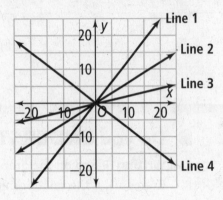

Similar:

Different:

Reflect

Is one line more different than the others? Explain.

_____

_____

_____

_____

Close and Check

Focus Question

What does it mean for an equation to be linear? What kind of relationships can be modeled by equations in the form $y = mx$?

_____

_____

_____

_____

Do you know HOW?

1. The graph shows the earnings e of an airplane mechanic for a number of weeks w at a constant rate r. Write an equation to model the situation shown.

Income

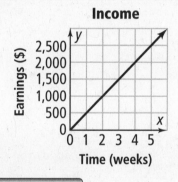

2. A machine manufactures a part in 11 minutes. A newer machine can manufacture the same part 1.5 minutes faster. Write an equation that models how many parts p each machine can manufacture in any number of minutes m.

Old Machine: [＿＿＿＿＿]

New Machine: [＿＿＿＿＿]

Do you UNDERSTAND?

3. Writing A diesel mechanic's earnings can be represented by the equation $e = 475w$. Who earns more, the airplane mechanic in Exercise 1 or the diesel mechanic? Explain.

_____

_____

_____

_____

4. Reasoning Are all proportional equations linear? Are all linear equations proportional? Explain.

_____

_____

_____

_____

_____

_____

The Slope of a Line

Common Core State Standards: 8.EE.5: Graph proportional relationships, interpreting the unit rate as the slope of the graph. Compare two different proportional relationships represented in different ways.

Launch

An architect diagrams a series of skyscrapers on a coordinate grid. Tell how they are alike and different.

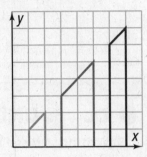

Alike:

Different:

Reflect

Is one building more different than the others? Explain.

_____

_____

_____

_____

Close and Check

Focus Question

What does the slope of a line tell you about the line?

_____

_____

_____

_____

▶ Do you know HOW?

1. What is the slope of the line?

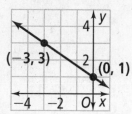

Slope: [ ]

2. What is the slope of the line that passes through the points (3, 3) and (1, −2)?

Slope: [ ]

3. Roof A has a rise of 11 and a run of 12. Roof B has a rise of 8 and a run of 9. Which roof is steeper?

[ ]

4. Climber A climbs at a rate of 14 feet every 3 minutes. Climber B climbs 19 feet in 4 minutes. Which climber has the faster rate?

[ ]

▶ Do you UNDERSTAND?

5. Reasoning What is the slope of a horizontal line? Choose two points and show how you determined your solution.

_____

_____

_____

_____

6. Error Analysis A classmate finds the slope of a line containing the points (−7, 5) and (−3, 9). Explain the error she made in her calculations and find the correct slope.

$$\frac{9-5}{-7-(-3)} = \frac{4}{-4} = -1$$

_____

_____

_____

_____

Unit Rates and Slope

Common Core State Standards: 8.EE.5: Graph proportional relationships, interpreting the unit rate as the slope of the graph. Compare two different proportional relationships represented in different ways.

Launch

The graph shows the results of a plant-growing contest among three friends at a local plant club.

Which friend's plant grew the fastest? Explain how you know.

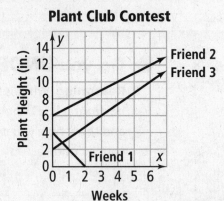

Reflect

Is one line more different than the others? Explain.

_____

_____

_____

_____

Close and Check

Do you know HOW?

1. A caterer is preparing meatloaf for a large party. She needs 3 eggs for 2 pounds of ground beef. Graph the ratio of eggs to ground beef.

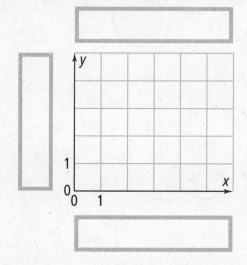

2. What is the slope of the line in the graph?

Slope:

3. Write an equation for Exercise 1 to find the number of eggs *y* for any number of pounds of ground beef *x*. How many eggs will be needed for 18 pounds of ground beef?

Equation:

_____ eggs

Do you UNDERSTAND?

4. Reasoning Your creative writing teacher says you will have 15 short stories due over the next 12 weeks. What is the slope of the graph of number of papers due? Explain whether the graph represents a proportional relationship.

5. Writing Explain how to graph a line if you only know one point on the line and the slope of the line.

Common Core State Standards: 8.EE.6: … derive the equation $y = mx$ for a line through the origin and the equation $y = mx + b$ for a line intercepting the vertical axis at b.

Launch

The graph shows the results of a plant-growing contest among three friends at a local plant club. The person with tallest plant after six weeks wins the contest.

Who won the contest? Do you think the contest was fair? Explain.

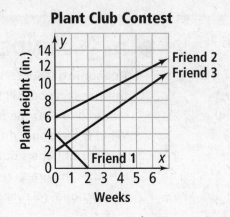

Plant Club Contest

Reflect

What do the lines all have in common?

_____

_____

_____

_____

Close and Check

Focus Question

What is the *y*-intercept of a graph? What does the *y*-intercept tell you about the equation being graphed?

_____

_____

_____

_____

▶ Do you know **HOW?**

1. You open a savings account with a $75 deposit. Then you deposit $25 each month. Complete the graph to model the situation.

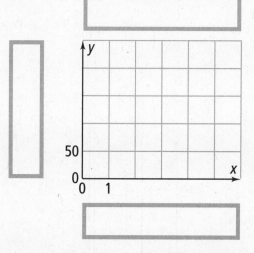

2. What does the *y*-intercept represent?

3. What is the slope of the line?

Slope:

4. What does the slope represent?

▶ Do you **UNDERSTAND?**

5. Compare and Contrast What about the graph in Exercise 1 would change if the initial deposit had been 0? What would stay the same? Explain.

_____

_____

_____

_____

_____

6. Error Analysis A classmate says a line with slope = 0 does not have a *y*-intercept. Do you agree? Explain.

_____

_____

_____

_____

_____

Linear Equations: $y = mx + b$

Common Core State Standards: 8.EE.6: ... derive the equation $y = mx$ for a line through the origin and the equation $y = mx + b$ for a line intercepting the vertical axis at b.

Launch

Complete the table. Describe any patterns you see between the slope and y-intercept for each line and the equation.

Equation	Slope	y-intercept
$y = 2x + 1$		
$y = 2x + 3$		
$y = -\frac{1}{3}x + 6$		
$y = x$		
$y = 1$		

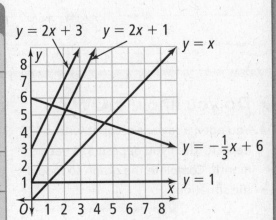

Reflect

Is it easier to spot the slope and y-intercept of a line from the graph or the equation of the line? Explain.

_____

_____

_____

_____

Close and Check

Focus Question

Previously you studied equations in the form $y = mx$. How are equations in the form $y = mx$ similar to equations in the form $y = mx + b$? How do you know when to use each form?

_____

_____

_____

_____

Do you know **HOW?**

Use the graph for Exercises 1–4.

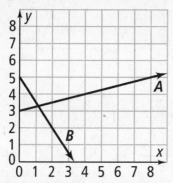

1. Write an equation in slope-intercept form for Line *A*.

2. Write an equation in slope-intercept form for Line *B*.

3. Graph and label Line *C* where $y = -\frac{2}{3}x + 7$.

4. Graph and label Line *D* where $y = \frac{7}{8}x + 1$.

Do you **UNDERSTAND?**

5. Reasoning You know the slope of a line and a point on the line that is not the *y*-intercept. Can you use a graph to write the equation of the line in slope-intercept form? Explain.

_____

_____

_____

_____

_____

_____

6. Writing Do the equations $y = \frac{5}{6}x + 2$ and $y = \frac{15}{18}x + 2$ represent two different lines? Explain.

_____

_____

_____

_____

_____

Problem Solving

Common Core State Standards: 8.EE.5: ... Compare two different proportional relationships represented in different ways. **8.EE.6:** ... derive the equation $y = mx$ for a line through the origin and the equation $y = mx + b$ for a line intercepting the vertical axis at b.

Launch

Create your own graph and matching linear equation. Describe a situation that makes sense for each representation. Label your graph appropriately. Your situation must include the point (2, 4).

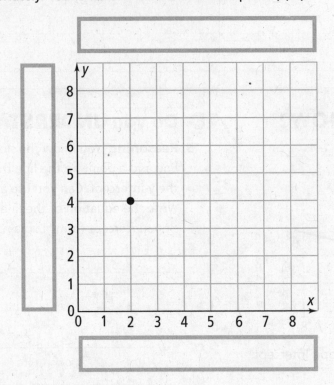

Equation:

Description of situation:

Reflect

What did you do first—write an equation, complete the graph, or describe the situation? Why?

_____

_____

_____

Close and Check

Focus Question

You have studied the relationship between linear equations and proportional relationships. How and when can you use linear equations to solve problems?

_____

_____

_____

_____

Do you know HOW?

1. To make a multi-age 800-meter race fair, Runner 1 gets a 100-meter head start. He runs 350 meters every 2 minutes. Represent on the graph how Runner 1 runs the race.

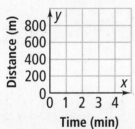
Runner 1

2. Runner 2 gets a 75-meter head start. Her rate is 210 meters per minute. Complete the table.

Time (min)	0	1	2	3	4
Distance (m)					

3. Runner 3 does not get a head start. He runs 750 meters every 3 minutes. Write an equation to represent Runner 3's distance y for x minutes.

[   ]

Do you UNDERSTAND?

4. Writing Which runner from Exercises 1–3 is ahead after 1 minute? Will that runner win the race? Explain.

_____

_____

_____

_____

_____

5. Reasoning Which is most helpful in problem solving, a graph, a table, or an equation? Explain.

_____

_____

_____

_____

_____

_____

What is a System of Linear Equations in Two Variables?

Common Core State Standards: 8.EE.8: Analyze and solve pairs of simultaneous linear equations.
8.EE.8.a: Understand that solutions to a system of two linear equations in two variables correspond to points of intersection of their graphs, ... Also, **8.EE.8.c.**

Launch

Two runners run a 40-yd dash at speeds shown in the diagram. Runner 1 starts 4 seconds before Runner 2 to make the race more competitive. Will Runner 2 pass Runner 1? Tell how you know.

Runner 1
4 yd/s

Runner 2
8 yd/s

Reflect

Do you think your method for solving the problem would be practical and easy to use for any race with runners who run any speed with any head start? Explain.

_____

_____

_____

_____

Close and Check

Focus Question

What does a system of linear equations allow you to describe? What does the solution of a system represent?

_____

_____

_____

_____

Do you know HOW?

1. Circle the systems of equations.

A. $7x - 5y = 16$ B. $2xy = 30$
                        $7x - 1 = 4y$

C. $y = 3x + 4$ D. $17 - xy$
   $y = 4x - 3$

2. Circle the ordered pair that is a solution to the system of equations.

$$2y + 6 = 3x$$
$$7x + 5 = 8y - 1$$

(4, 3)   (4, 4)   (6, 6)   (8, 9)

3. The table shows the initial height and growth rate of an apple tree and a cherry tree. Write a system of equations the gardener could use to determine the time t when height h of the two trees will be the same.

	Apple	Cherry
Initial Height (ft)	2.75	2.12
Growth Rate (ft/yr)	1.2	1.38

Do you UNDERSTAND?

4. Writing Two brothers decide to save money. One starts with $10, and saves $2 each day. The other starts with none, but saves $3 each day. What can a system of equations tell you about the situation?

_____

_____

_____

_____

5. Error Analysis A classmate uses the system of equations below to conclude that (2, 5) is a solution because $(3 \cdot 2) + (2 \cdot 5) = 16$. Explain why she is incorrect.

$$3x + 2y = 16$$
$$-xy + 5 = 15$$

_____

_____

_____

_____

Estimating Solutions of Linear Systems by Inspection

Common Core State Standards: 8.EE.8: Analyze and solve pairs of simultaneous linear equations.
8.EE.8.b: Solve systems of two linear equations in two variables algebraically, and estimate solutions by graphing the equations. Solve simple cases by inspection ... .

Launch

Two runners run a 100-yd dash at speeds shown in the diagram. Runner 3 starts 4 seconds before Runner 2. Will Runner 2 pass Runner 3? Tell how you know.

Runner 3
8 yd/s

Runner 2
8 yd/s

Reflect

Do you need to set up a system of equations to solve the problem? Explain.

_____

_____

_____

_____

Close and Check

How can you find the solution of a system of linear equations just by inspecting the equations?

_____

_____

_____

_____

Do you know HOW?

1. Circle the system of equations that has no solution.

A. $y = 3x - 3$ B. $2y = 7x + 2$

$\frac{y}{3} = x - 1$ $y = 3.5x + 2$

C. $2x - 5y = 7x + 5$ D. $y = 5x + 7$

     $y = x - 1$ $y = -5x + 7$

2. Circle the correct description of the system of equations.

$$16x + 4 = 8y - 1$$
$$3x + 0.5 = y$$

A. one solution

B. no solution

C. infinite number of solutions

3. Which equation does NOT complete the system of equations with an infinite number of solutions?

$$6x + 3y = 18$$

A. $2x + y = 6$

B. $y = -2x + 6$

C. $-y = -2x - 6$

D. $2y = -4x + 12$

Do you UNDERSTAND?

4. Writing Explain how to analyze a system of equations using the point-slope form of the equations of two lines.

_____

_____

_____

_____

_____

_____

5. Error Analysis A classmate concludes that the system of equations in Exercise 1D has infinitely many solutions. Explain why this is not true.

_____

_____

_____

_____

_____

Solving Systems of Linear Equations by Graphing

Common Core State Standards: 8.EE.8.a: Understand that solutions to a system of two linear equations … correspond to points of intersection of their graphs …. **8.EE.8.b:** … estimate solutions by graphing the equations. Also, **8.EE.8, 8.EE.8.c.**

Launch

Spy 1 and Spy 2 hand off secret documents at point (1, 3), a park bench. Each spy walks past the bench in a different straight line so they can't be easily tracked.

Show each path by writing an equation and drawing them on the graph. Label each spy's path on the graph.

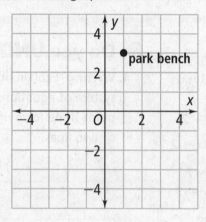

Reflect

Did you write the equations or draw the paths first? Explain why.

_____

_____

_____

_____

Close and Check

Focus Question

How can a graph help you find the solution of a system of linear equations?

_____

_____

_____

_____

Do you know **HOW?**

1. What is the solution of the system represented by the graph?

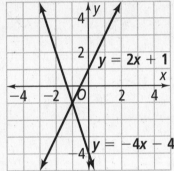

2. Estimate the solution of the system by graphing the equations.

$$3y = 2x + 1$$
$$-3y + 6x = 3$$

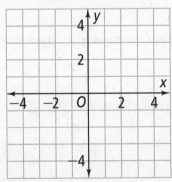

Do you **UNDERSTAND?**

3. Writing A GameSwap membership costs $20 and includes one game a month for $5. Non-members can get one game a month for $7. Explain how to use this information to decide whether to become a member.

_____

_____

_____

_____

_____

4. Error Analysis A friend uses a graph to compare her commute to school with yours. She says the point at which the two lines intersect is when you both arrive at school. Is she correct? Explain.

_____

_____

_____

_____

Solving Systems of Linear Equations Using Substitution

Common Core State Standards: 8.EE.8.b: Solve systems of two linear equations in two variables algebraically, and estimate solutions by graphing the equations. **8.EE.8.c:** Solve real-world and mathematical problems leading to two linear equations in two variables. Also, **8.EE.8.**

Launch

Solve the system of equations shown. Tell what you did.

$$y = x \qquad 3x - 2y = 3$$

Reflect

What does the equal sign mean? How does that affect how you solve this problem?

_____

_____

_____

_____

Close and Check

Focus Question

Some systems cannot be solved by graphing. How can you use algebra to solve a system?

_____

_____

_____

_____

Do you know HOW?

1. What is the solution of the system? Use substitution.

$$4x - y = 25$$
$$3y - 2 = x$$

2. An air conditioner cools the inside of your home as it gets warmer outside. Use the table to write and solve a system of equations to determine the hour h when the temperatures t will be the same.

	Inside	Outside
Initial Temperature	77°F	65°F
Rate of Change	−1°F/hr	2°F/hr

System:

Solution:

Do you UNDERSTAND?

3. Reasoning What is the meaning of the solution to Exercise 2?

_____

_____

_____

_____

_____

4. Writing Why is it more accurate to solve a system of equations containing decimals by using algebra and substitution than by graphing the equations?

_____

_____

_____

_____

_____

_____

_____

Solving Systems of Linear Equations Using Addition

Common Core State Standards: 8.EE.8.b: Solve systems of two linear equations in two variables algebraically, and estimate solutions by graphing the equations. **8.EE.8.c:** Solve real-world and mathematical problems leading to two linear equations in two variables. Also, **8.EE.8, 8.EE.8.a.**

Launch

Each piece of paper shows a numerical expression or an algebraic expression. Can you show the same total value using fewer pieces of paper? Write your expressions and explain your reasoning.

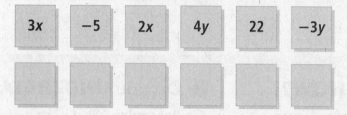

Reflect

How does equality help you solve this problem?

_____

_____

_____

_____

Close and Check

> ### Focus Question
> What kinds of systems are easiest to solve using addition?
>
> _____
>
> _____
>
> _____
>
> _____

▶ Do you know **HOW?**

1. Solve the system of equations using addition.

$$6x + 4y = 42$$
$$3x - 4y = 3$$

2. A delivery truck's route is 588 miles long. The first part of the route 148 miles longer than the second part. What is the distance of each part?

First Part: [   ]   Second Part: [   ]

3. There are 2,250 students enrolled in the middle school and high school. The middle school has 374 less students than the high school. How many students are enrolled in each school?

Middle School: [   ]   High School: [   ]

▶ Do you **UNDERSTAND?**

4. Compare and Contrast Does it make a difference if a system is solved using the substitution method or the addition method? Explain.

_____

_____

_____

_____

5. Error Analysis A classmate says the system cannot be solved using the addition method. Explain how to solve this system using the addition method.

$$4x + 2y = 5y + 7$$
$$8x + 3y = 41$$

_____

_____

_____

_____

_____

Solving Systems of Linear Equations Using Subtraction

Common Core State Standards: 8.EE.8: Analyze and solve pairs of simultaneous linear equations.
8.EE.8.b: Solve systems of two linear equations in two variables algebraically … . **8.EE.8.c:** Solve …
problems leading to two linear equations in two variables … . Also, **8.EE.8.a**

Launch

Each friend has the same amount of money. Envelope x has one amount of money. Envelope y has a different amount of money.

Provide a possible amount of money for envelopes x and y. Tell how you decided.

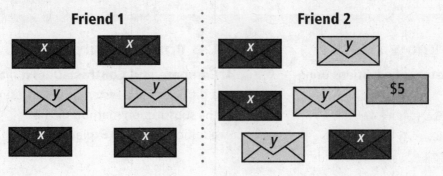

Reflect

Does this problem have one answer? Explain.

_____

_____

_____

_____

Close and Check

Focus Question

What kinds of systems are easiest to solve using subtraction?

_____

_____

_____

_____

Do you know HOW?

1. Circle the system of equations that would be solved most efficiently by using the subtraction method.

A. $x = 4y - 12$
   $x = 2(3y + 8)$

B. $7r + 2s = 18$
   $5r - 9 = 2s$

C. $6p + 2q = 4$
   $4p + 2q = 2$

D. $9a + 8b = 15$
   $3a - 8b = 5$

2. Solve the system of equations by using subtraction.

$$7s + 2t = 31$$
$$5s + 2t = 25$$

3. The 8th grade class sells 275 magazine subscriptions and individual greeting cards for a fundraiser. The subscriptions cost $26 and cards cost $1 each. The students earn $2,875. How many of each item is sold?

Magazines: Greeting Cards:

Do you UNDERSTAND?

4. Reasoning Your friend says he would solve this system of equations by using the subtraction method. Why might that method be efficient in this case?

$$12x - 5y = 73$$
$$10x - 5y = 35$$

_____

_____

_____

_____

_____

5. Compare and Contrast Explain how to determine whether the addition method or the subtraction method is most efficient for solving a system of equations.

_____

_____

_____

_____

_____

Problem Solving

Common Core State Standards: 8.EE.8.b: Solve systems of two linear equations in two variables algebraically, and estimate solutions by graphing the equations. **8.EE.8.c:** Solve real-world and mathematical problems leading to two linear equations in two variables. Also, **8.EE.8.**

Launch

In each account, the sum of the envelopes results in the balance shown. You can take either the x envelopes or the y envelopes from each account. Use systems of equations to show which envelope type you would take.

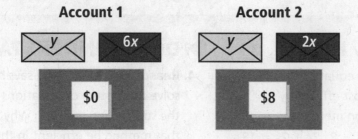

Account 1   **Account 2**

y $6x$ y $2x$

$0 $8

Reflect

In the real world, what do you think each envelope could represent?

_____

_____

_____

_____

Close and Check

Focus Question

In this topic, you learned how to solve systems of two linear equations in two variables using different methods. How do you build a solution strategy for a system of equations when the method of solving is left up to you?

_____

_____

_____

_____

Do you know HOW?

1. Write *substitution, addition,* or *subtraction* to tell which method is most efficient for finding the solution.

   A. $9j + 4k = 17$
   $5j + 4k = 13$

   B. $y = 7x - 3$
   $y = 6x + 5$

   C. $8v + 2w = 28$
   $5v - 2w = 23$

2. Solve the system of equations by multiplying one or both equations by a constant.

   $2a + 5b = 53$
   $8a - 3b = 5$

3. A store offers pens for $4/pack and day planners for $8 each. You spend $48 on these items. The next week the items go on sale. Pens cost $2/pack and day planners cost $6 each. The same purchase now costs $30. How many of each item did you buy?

   Packs of Pens: Day Planners:

Do you UNDERSTAND?

4. **Writing** How can solving systems of equations be helpful in real-life problem solving?

   _____

   _____

   _____

   _____

   _____

5. **Error Analysis** You have 3 coins and 4 bills totaling $16.75. Your friend has 12 coins and 3 bills totaling $7.98. Your friend says she can use a system of equations to figure out what bills and coins you have. What is the error in her reasoning?

   _____

   _____

   _____

   _____

Recognizing a Function

Common Core State Standards: 8.F.1: Understand that a function is a rule that assigns to each input exactly one output. The graph of a function is the set of ordered pairs consisting of an input and the corresponding output.

Launch

Two local dog-walking services scratch and claw for customers using sometimes unusual pay plans.

Which service would you use if you need a dog break for 2 hours on Friday, 3 hours on Saturday, and 1 hour on Sunday? Why?

Friendly Dog Walking

Flip-a-Coin Fees

1 hour $2 or $4

2 hours $3 or $6

3 hours $6 or $8

Dog Walk Friends

Fees

1 hour $3

2 hours $5

3 hours $7

Reflect

Do companies usually have set prices or prices that can vary? Why?

_____

_____

_____

_____

Close and Check

Focus Question

How will you know a function when you see one?

_____

_____

_____

_____

Do you know HOW?

1. Name the set of ordered pairs represented by the mapping diagram.

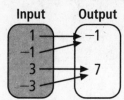

Input   Output

_____

2. Complete the table for the set of ordered pairs.

{(4, 2), (4, −2), (9, 3), (9, −3)}

Input				
Output				

3. Circle the sets of ordered pairs that represent a function.

A. {(0, 2), (1, −2), (2, 3), (4, −3)}

B. {(4, 0), (4, 4), (4, 8), (4, 12)}

C. {(2, 6), (4, 6), (6, 6), (6, 8)}

D. {(5, −5), (4, −4), (3, −3), (2, −2)}

Do you UNDERSTAND?

4. Writing Is the set of ordered pairs in Exercise 2 a function? Explain.

_____

_____

_____

5. Reasoning Based on the graph, does this set of points represent a function? Explain.

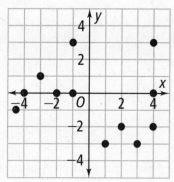

_____

_____

_____

_____

_____

Representing a Function

Common Core State Standards: 8.F.1: Understand that a function is a rule that assigns to each input exactly one output. The graph of a function is the set of ordered pairs consisting of an input and the corresponding output.

Launch

Write some of the ordered pairs in the table to make a function.
Describe what the function could mean.

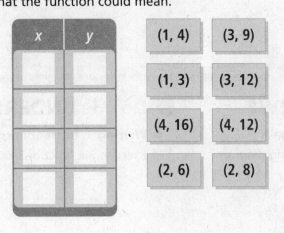

x	y

(1, 4)   (3, 9)

(1, 3)   (3, 12)

(4, 16)   (4, 12)

(2, 6)   (2, 8)

Reflect

Name two ordered pairs that cannot belong to the same function. Explain.

_____

_____

_____

_____

Close and Check

Focus Question

There are several ways to represent functions. What are the advantages of each of these ways?

_____

_____

_____

_____

Do you know HOW?

1. The earth travels 30 km/s in its orbit around the sun. Circle the correct representation(s) of this situation.

A. $30x = y$

B. $\{(0, 0), (1, 30), (3, 60)\}$

C.

x	y
1	30
4	120
7	210
10	300

D.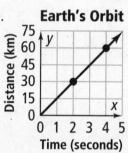

Earth's Orbit

2. Complete the table of values for $y = 3x - 2$.

x	y
0	
4	
7	
9	

Do you UNDERSTAND?

3. Reasoning Consider a circle graphed on the coordinate plane with the center of the circle at the origin. Can the equation of a circle ever be a function? Explain.

_____

_____

_____

_____

_____

4. Writing A friend says the equation $\sqrt{x} = y$ is not an example of a function because if $x = 16$, then $y = -4$ and 4. Explain whether this reasoning is always correct.

_____

_____

_____

_____

_____

7-3 Linear Functions

Common Core State Standards: 8.F.3: Interpret the equation … as defining a linear function, whose graph is a straight line … . **8.F.5:** Describe qualitatively the functional relationship between two quantities by analyzing a graph (e.g., where the function is … linear or nonlinear).

Launch

Draw lines to sort the graphs into two groups. Describe each of your groups.

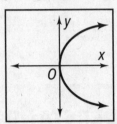 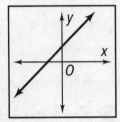 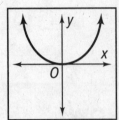 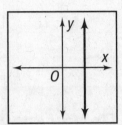

Group 1   **Group 2**

Reflect

Could you have sorted the graphs in a different way? Explain.

_____

_____

_____

_____

7-3 Linear Functions

Common Core State Standards: 8.F.3: Interpret the equation … as defining a linear function, whose graph is a straight line … . **8.F.5:** Describe qualitatively the functional relationship between two quantities by analyzing a graph (e.g., where the function is … linear or nonlinear).

Launch

Draw lines to sort the graphs into two groups. Describe each of your groups.

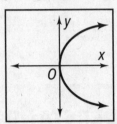 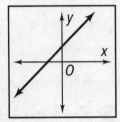 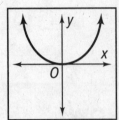 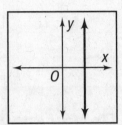

Group 1   **Group 2**

Reflect

Could you have sorted the graphs in a different way? Explain.

_____

_____

_____

_____

Copyright © by Pearson Education, Inc., or its affiliates. All Rights Reserved.

Topic 7   78   Lesson 7-3

Close and Check

> ### Focus Question
> What are linear functions? How are linear functions useful?
>
> _____
>
> _____
>
> _____
>
> _____

▶ Do you know **HOW?**

1. Graph the set of ordered pairs.

{(−3, −4), (−2, −2), (−1, 0), (0, 2), (1, 4)}

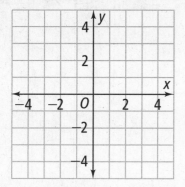

2. Do the ordered pairs in Exercise 1 represent a function?

3. Find the rate of change in the table.

Input	Output
−3	−5
−1	1
1	7
3	13

▶ Do you **UNDERSTAND?**

4. Writing An ordered pair with the x-coordinate 2 is added to the set in Exercise 1. Explain how to find the y-coordinate of the ordered pair.

_____

_____

_____

_____

5. Error Analysis What mistake did your classmate make in determining the rate of change in the table below? Find the actual rate of change.

Input	Output	Rate of change = +6
−5	1	−5 + 6 = 1
−2	4	−2 + 6 = 4
1	7	1 + 6 = 7

_____

_____

_____

Nonlinear Functions

Common Core State Standards: 8.F.3: Interpret the equation ... is a straight line; give examples of functions that are not linear. **8.F.5:** Describe qualitatively the functional relationship between two quantities by analyzing a graph (e.g., where the function is ... linear or nonlinear). Also, **8.F.1.**

Launch

Your friend designs a rectangular board game using 16 square pieces. Let x equal the number of rows of squares on the board and y equal the number of columns on the board.

Do the numbers of rows and columns represent a function? A linear function? Use a table or a graph to support your response.

Reflect

Did you choose to support your response with a table or a graph? Explain your choice.

_____

_____

_____

_____

Close and Check

Focus Question

How do nonlinear functions differ from linear functions?

_____

_____

_____

_____

Do you know **HOW?**

1. Circle the graph(s) that represent a nonlinear function.

A.   B.

C.   D.

2. Complete the table of values for the equation $|x| - 2 = y$.

x	y
−2	
−1	
0	
1	
2	

Do you **UNDERSTAND?**

3. Writing Does the table in Exercise 2 represent a linear function? Explain.

_____

_____

_____

_____

_____

_____

4. Error Analysis A classmate says the equation $y = \frac{5}{3}x - 6$ is nonlinear. Do you agree? Explain.

_____

_____

_____

_____

_____

_____

Increasing and Decreasing Intervals

Common Core State Standards: 8.F.5: Describe qualitatively the functional relationship between two quantities by analyzing a graph (e.g., where the function is increasing or decreasing). Sketch a graph that exhibits the qualitative features of a function that has been described verbally.

Launch

The graph represents the number of people in an outdoor stadium for a baseball game. Tell what the *x*- and *y*-axes represent. Tell what happens during parts A to E to the people at the game.

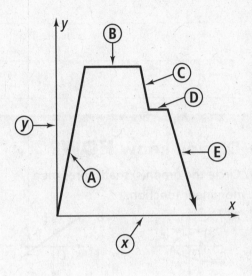

x:

y:

A:

B:

C:

D:

E:

Reflect

How could a graph such as this be valuable to the owners of the baseball team? Explain.

_____

_____

_____

_____

Close and Check

Focus Question

How does a graph describe the functional relationship between two quantities?

_____

_____

_____

_____

Do you know HOW?

1. List the type of intervals on the graph by writing the letters under the correct heading below.

Sales Trends

Increasing   Constant   Decreasing

2. Does the graph show more increasing or decreasing intervals?

3. What was the total change in income from the beginning of March through the end of April?

4. What was the total change in income from the beginning of March through the end of May?

Do you UNDERSTAND?

5. Reasoning Explain why intervals c and d in Exercise 1 are labeled separately rather than as one interval.

_____

_____

_____

_____

_____

_____

6. Writing Explain what the intervals b and f in Exercise 1 represent.

_____

_____

_____

_____

_____

_____

Sketching a Function Graph

Common Core State Standards: 8.F.5: Describe qualitatively the functional relationship between two quantities by analyzing a graph (e.g., where the function is increasing or decreasing). Sketch a graph that exhibits the qualitative features of a function that has been described verbally.

Launch

Your cousin keeps the hot dog supply stocked at a concession stand at the baseball game. Despite lots of hungry fans, the stand never runs out of hot hot dogs.

Sketch one possible graph of your cousin's efforts on the coordinate grid. Label the x- and y-axes and tell why your graph makes sense.

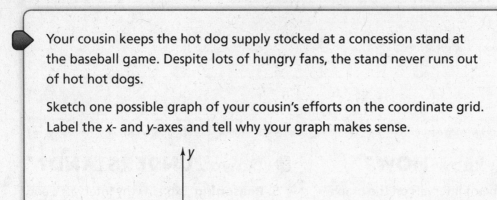

Reflect

How could your cousin use a graph like the one you created?

_____

_____

_____

_____

Close and Check

Focus Question

How does sketching the graph of a function help you to determine the behavior of a function?

_____

_____

_____

_____

Do you know HOW?

Write the letter of the graph that matches each description in Exercises 1–3.

Graph A   **Graph B**   **Graph C**

1. A car starts from a complete stop and accelerates at a constant rate. Then it travels at a constant speed until the driver sees a stop sign and gradually slows down to a stop.

2. A car is traveling at a constant speed. It accelerates at a constant rate. Finally, it continues traveling at a constant speed.

3. A car slows down at a constant speed as it approaches a red light. After a short time, the light changes and the car gradually accelerates.

Do you UNDERSTAND?

4. **Writing** Sketch a graph, and then write a brief description of what the graph could represent.

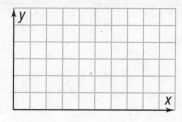

_____

_____

_____

_____

5. **Reasoning** Is it possible for a sketch of a graph to represent more than one situation? Explain.

_____

_____

_____

_____

_____

Problem Solving

Common Core State Standards: 8.F.5: Describe qualitatively the functional relationship between two quantities by analyzing a graph (e.g., where the function is increasing or decreasing). Sketch a graph that exhibits the qualitative features of a function that has been described verbally.

Launch

The graphs represent ticket sales for three upcoming games with x representing time and y the rate of ticket sales.

Which game will be the easiest for your cousin to plan how many hot dog buns to buy? Which game will be the most challenging to plan for? Explain why.

Graph A   **Graph B**   **Graph C**

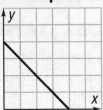  

Easiest:

Most Challenging:

Reflect

What value do the graphs have for your cousin? What other information might he want to make his plans?

_____

_____

_____

_____

Close and Check

Focus Question

How can you use different representations of a function to analyze a situation?

_____

_____

_____

_____

Do you know HOW?

1. Complete the table. Is the equation linear or nonlinear?

$$x^3 - 3 = y$$

x	y
−1	
0	
1	
2	

[   ]

2. Graph the equation from Exercise 1. Is the equation a function?

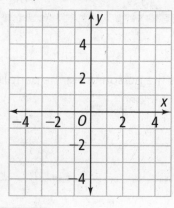

[   ]

Do you UNDERSTAND?

3. Writing Explain how you determined whether the equation in Exercise 1 is linear or nonlinear.

_____

_____

_____

_____

4. Reasoning An interior designer wants to show her customers how the length of a square wall determines the total area. She uses the equation $x^2 = y$. Would you use the equation, a table, or a graph to share with the customers? Explain.

_____

_____

_____

_____

_____

Defining a Linear Function Rule

Common Core State Standards: 8.F.3: Interpret the equation $y = mx + b$ as defining a linear function, whose graph is a straight line …. **8.F.4:** Construct a function to model a linear relationship between two quantities …. Also, **8.F.1** and **8.F.5**.

Launch

Draw a line to the graph that could represent each situation.

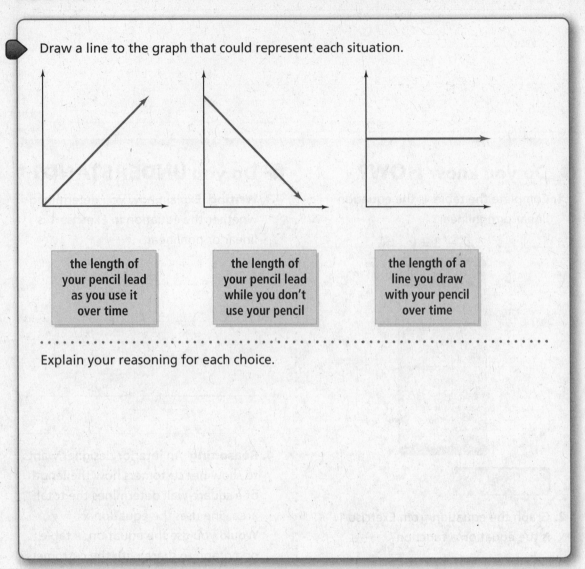

the length of your pencil lead as you use it over time

the length of your pencil lead while you don't use your pencil

the length of a line you draw with your pencil over time

Explain your reasoning for each choice.

Reflect

Think of the graphs where the pencil lead is being used. Is the person using the pencil at a constant rate or stopping and starting a lot? Explain your thinking.

_____

_____

_____

_____

Close and Check

Focus Question

How can you define or describe a linear function?

_____

_____

_____

Do you know **HOW?**

1. What linear function rule describes the graph?

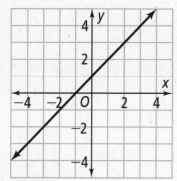

2. Circle each linear function rule.

$y = 4x^2$

$y = x - 7$

$y = -\left(\frac{x}{9}\right)$

$y = 12 + \frac{2}{x}$

3. You earn an allowance of $5 each week. You earn additional money m for helping others in the neighborhood. Write a function rule to find the total income i you can earn in one week.

Do you **UNDERSTAND?**

4. Error Analysis Your friend can jump rope 32 times in one minute. She writes a rule to predict how many times she can jump for other time periods.

$$j = 32 + m$$
$$j = \text{jumps} \quad m = \text{minutes}$$

Explain her error and write the correct equation.

_____

_____

_____

_____

5. Reasoning A man in a 5K race runs 1 km and then walks 0.5 km. If the man continues this pattern for the entire race, is the graph of his distance over time linear? Explain.

_____

_____

_____

_____

Rate of Change

Common Core State Standards: 8.F.4: ... Determine the rate of change and initial value of the function from a description of a relationship or from two (x, y) values ... . Interpret the rate of change and initial value of a linear function in terms of the situation it models ... . Also, **8.F.5.**

Launch

Your friend walks from the bus stop to her favorite museum. She first walks one or more blocks along a street, then one or more blocks along an avenue. She continues this pattern until she reaches the museum, taking the shortest path possible.

Draw and describe her walking pattern.

Drawing   **Description**

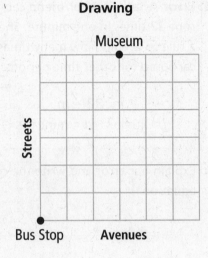

Reflect

Suppose your friend could fly directly from the bus stop to the museum. How would the flight path compare with her walking path?

_____

_____

_____

_____

Close and Check

Focus Question

Each part of a linear function plays a role in how its graph looks. What role does the rate of change play?

_____

_____

_____

_____

Do you know HOW?

1. A board is placed over the stairs of a store to allow wheelchair access. What is the rate of change of the linear function that models the height of the ramp?

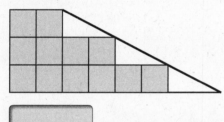

2. What is the rate of change of the linear function $y = -\frac{1}{7}x + 4$?

3. Find the rate of change for the data in the table as a unit rate.

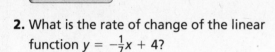

Hours	3	5	7
Earnings	$20.25	$33.75	$47.25

Do you UNDERSTAND?

4. Reasoning What does the rate of change mean in Exercise 3?

_____

_____

_____

5. Writing Explain how to use the table to determine the rate of change.

Customers	CDs Sold
20	24
30	36
40	48

_____

_____

_____

_____

_____

Initial Value

Common Core State Standards: 8.F.4: ... Determine the rate of change and initial value of the function ... . Interpret the rate of change and initial value of a linear function in terms of the situation it models ... . Also, 8.F.3 and 8.F.5.

Launch

At a school craft fair, you sell T-shirts of your own design for $6 each. You bring money with you to make change. After selling 5 T-shirts, you have $44.

How much money did you bring to make change? Show your solution in a table or graph and explain your reasoning.

Reflect

Why didn't you have $0 when you had not sold a T-shirt?

_____

_____

_____

_____

Close and Check

▶ Focus Question

Each part of a linear function plays a role in how its graph looks. What role does the initial value play?

_____

_____

_____

_____

▶ Do you know HOW?

1. What is the initial value of the linear function $y = 5x - 6$?

2. The graph below shows the outside temperature for several hours in one day. Write each value and the equation of the linear function.

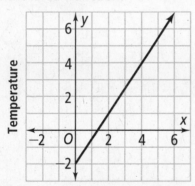

Time

rate of change:

initial value: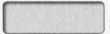

function rule: [   ]

▶ Do you UNDERSTAND?

3. Reasoning Explain what the initial value and the rate of change mean in Exercise 2.

_____

_____

_____

_____

4. Error Analysis A student looks at the graph below and says that the rate of change is $\frac{2}{1}$ and the initial value is 2. Explain why this is incorrect.

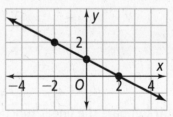

_____

_____

_____

_____

Comparing Two Linear Functions

Common Core State Standards: 8.F.2: Compare properties of two functions each represented in a different way (algebraically, graphically, numerically in tables, or by verbal descriptions).

Launch

The city's second-best scientist knew his Robot Blue was too slow to beat Robot Red in a 100-yard race. So, he rigged the race to make it end in a tie.

How did the scientist rig the race? How much faster than Robot Blue does Robot Red run?

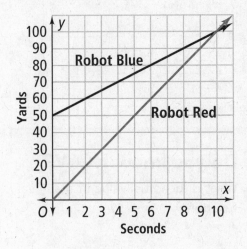

Reflect

When you compare the linear functions of the two robots on the graph, what are you comparing?

_____

_____

_____

_____

Close and Check

Focus Question

How can you compare linear functions? Why would you want to?

_____

_____

_____

_____

Do you know HOW?

1. Circle the two linear functions of the lines that do not intersect.

$y = \frac{1}{4}x + 5$ $y = \frac{4}{1}x - 5$

$y = \frac{1}{4}x - 5$ $y = -\frac{4}{1}x + 5$

Use the graph below to answer Exercises 2 and 3.

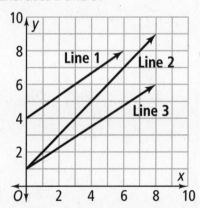

2. Which two lines have the same rate of change?

Lines [ ] and [ ]

3. Which two lines have the same initial value?

Lines [ ] and [ ]

Do you UNDERSTAND?

4. Reasoning Two linear functions have the same rate of change and the same initial value. What do you know about the graph of the two lines? Explain.

_____

_____

_____

_____

5. Writing You sell 7 tickets to the school play to your family. Your friend sells 4 tickets to her family. On Saturday, your friend sells twice as many tickets as you. Describe the graphs of these ticket sales.

_____

_____

_____

_____

Constructing a Function to Model a Linear Relationship

Common Core State Standards: 8.F.4: Construct a function to model a linear relationship between two quantities .... Interpret the rate of change and initial value of a linear function in terms of the situation it models, and in terms of its graph or a table of values.

Launch

The equation, the table, and the graph each represent the same functional relationship. Make up a real-world situation that matches this function. Tell how it matches.

$y = 2x + 10$

Input	Output
0	10
2	14
4	18
6	22
8	26
10	30

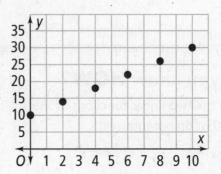

Reflect

Which representation was most helpful in thinking of a situation—the equation, the table, or the graph? Explain.

_____

_____

_____

_____

Close and Check

Focus Question

What do you need to know to write a linear function rule?

_____

_____

_____

Do you know HOW?

1. A box office is selling concert tickets for $5 each.

   Write a function rule to model the price p for any number of tickets t.

   [ ]

2. The same box office offers buttons with pictures of the band with the purchase of any ticket. You pay $6 for a ticket and 1 button, while your friend pays $8 for a ticket and 3 buttons.

   Write a function rule to model the price p for a ticket and any number of buttons b.

   [ ]

3. The box office decides to charge a service fee of $1.75 for each transaction.

   Write a function rule to model the new price p for any number of tickets t.

   [ ]

Do you UNDERSTAND?

4. **Compare and Contrast** Tell what is the same and what is different about the graphs of the following function rules.

   $$y = 3x + 5 \quad \text{and} \quad y = -3x + 5$$

   _____

   _____

   _____

   _____

   _____

   _____

5. **Writing** Explain how it is possible to write the linear function rule for a line by using the point and the rate of change given below.

   $$(0, -6); \, m = \frac{3}{4}$$

   _____

   _____

   _____

   _____

   _____

Problem Solving

Common Core State Standards: 8.F.4: Construct a function to model a linear relationship between two quantities .... Interpret the rate of change and initial value of a linear function in terms of the situation it models, and in terms of its graph or a table of values.

Launch

The city's second-best scientist makes 95 Robot Blues. He sells them only in boxes of 4 robots each and waits for orders.

After how many orders will the scientist have to make more robots?
Use a table, graph, or equation to support your answer.

Reflect

How does the graph, table, or equation help you solve the problem?

_____

_____

_____

_____

Close and Check

Focus Question

How are linear functions useful?

_____

_____

_____

_____

▶ Do you know HOW?

1. At $t = 0$, a sudden downpour of rain begins to fall at a constant rate. After 15 minutes, 1.5 inches of rain has fallen. Later during the storm, you check the rain gauge. How long has it been raining when you check the gauge?

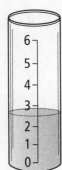

 minutes

2. The rain suddenly stops 30 minutes after it began. How much total rain has fallen?

[   ] inches

▶ Do you UNDERSTAND?

3. Error Analysis The data in the table was used to write the linear function rule $y = -x + 5$. Explain the error in the function rule.

Grade	Age
?	3
1	6
4	9
7	12

_____

_____

_____

4. Writing How can understanding the meaning of the parts of a linear function rule be helpful when evaluating the positive and negative solutions of a function?

_____

_____

_____

_____

Translations

Common Core Standards: 8.G.1: Verify … properties of … translations: **8.G.1.a:** Lines are taken to lines … segments to … segments … . **8.G.1.b:** Angles … to angles … . **8.G.1.c:** Parallel lines … to parallel lines. **8.G.3:** Describe the effect of dilations … and reflections … using coordinates.

Launch

Your friend begins building a figure out of shapes. He traces a trapezoid, slides it, traces one side, and then strangely stops.

Complete the tracing of the trapezoid to show your friend's slide. Explain why your tracing shows the slide.

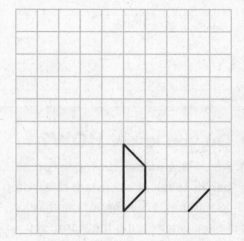

How my friend slid the trapezoid:

How my tracing shows the slide:

Reflect

Were there parallel line segments in the trapezoid before the slide? What about after the slide? Tell how you know.

_____

_____

_____

_____

Close and Check

Focus Question

What effect does a slide have on a figure?

_____

_____

_____

_____

Do you know HOW?

1. The vertices of △XYZ are X(−4, 1), Y(2, 2), and Z(−1, −1). If you translate △XYZ 3 units left and 1 unit down, what are the coordinates of Y′?

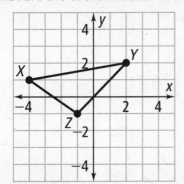

2. Use arrow notation to write a rule that describes the translation shown.

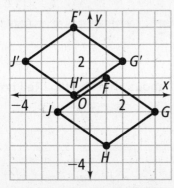

Do you UNDERSTAND?

3. Reasoning How do you know whether to add or subtract units from x and y when using arrow notation to describe a translation?

_____

_____

_____

_____

4. Error Analysis Explain the error in the translation below.

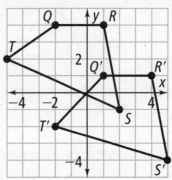

_____

_____

_____

_____

Reflections

Common Core Standards: 8.G.1: Verify ... properties of ... reflections ... : **8.G.1.a:** Lines are taken to lines ... segments to ... segments ... . **8.G.1.b:** Angles ... to angles ... . **8.G.1.c:** Parallel lines ... to parallel lines. **8.G.3:** Describe the effect of dilations ... and reflections ... using coordinates.

Launch

Your friend continues the figure. He traces a triangle, flips it over his pencil, traces one side, and then suddenly ceases.

Complete the triangle tracing to show your friend's flip. Explain why your tracing shows the flip.

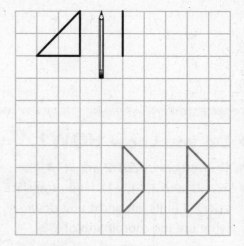

How my friend flipped the triangle:

How my tracing shows the flip:

Reflect

Is there a right angle in the triangle before the flip? What about after the flip? Tell how you know.

_____

_____

_____

_____

Close and Check

Focus Question

What effect does a flip have on a figure?

_____

_____

_____

_____

Do you know **HOW?**

1. The vertices of quadrilateral *QRST* are $Q(-1, 3)$, $R(2, 2)$, $S(3, -2)$, $T(1, -2)$. Graph quadrilateral *QRST* and quadrilateral *Q'R'S'T'*, its image after a reflection across the *x*-axis.

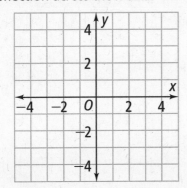

2. Use arrow notation to show how *QRST* maps to *Q'R'S'T'* from Exercise 1.

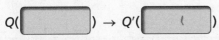

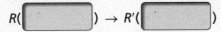

$Q(\boxed{}) \rightarrow Q'(\boxed{})$

$R(\boxed{}) \rightarrow R'(\boxed{})$

$S(\boxed{}) \rightarrow S'(\boxed{})$

$T(\boxed{}) \rightarrow T'(\boxed{})$

Do you **UNDERSTAND?**

3. Compare and Contrast How are translations and reflections the same and different?

_____

_____

_____

_____

4. Error Analysis A classmate says that the reflection across the *x*-axis of $\triangle PQR$ is $\triangle P'Q'R'$ where $P'(-2, 1)$, $Q'(-5, -2)$, and $R'(2, -4)$. What error did he make? What should the vertices be?

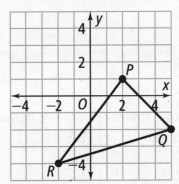

_____

_____

_____

Rotations

Common Core Standards: 8.G.1: Verify … properties of rotations … : **8.G.1.a:** Lines are taken to lines … segments to … segments … . **8.G.1.b:** Angles … to angles … . **8.G.1.c:** Parallel lines … to parallel lines. **8.G.3:** Describe the effect of dilations … and reflections … using coordinates.

Launch

Your friend nearly completes his figure. He traces a square, turns it, traces one side, and then curiously quits.

Complete the turn and tracing of the square. Explain why your tracing shows your friend's turn.

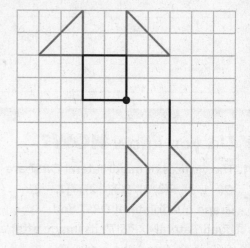

How my friend turned the square:

How my tracing shows the turn:

Reflect

What other transformations could your friend have used to move the square to the same position?

_____

_____

_____

_____

Close and Check

Do you know HOW?

1. Use arrow notation to show how △JKL maps to its image after a rotation 180° about the origin.

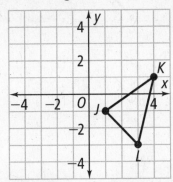

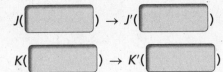

J([   ]) → J'([   ])

K([   ]) → K'([   ])

L([   ]) → L'([   ])

2. The vertices of parallelogram *WXYZ* are $W(-1, 1)$, $X(3, 2)$, $Y(3, -1)$, $Z(-1, -2)$. The vertices of its image, parallelogram *W'X'Y'Z'*, are $W'(-1, 1)$, $X'(3, 2)$, $Y'(3, -1)$, $Z'(-1, -2)$. What is the angle of rotation?

[   ]

Do you UNDERSTAND?

3. Compare and Contrast How are reflections and rotations the same and different?

_____

_____

_____

_____

_____

4. Reasoning Would the relationship between the vertices of any figure rotated 360° and its image always be true regardless of the point of rotation? Explain.

_____

_____

_____

_____

_____

Congruent Figures

Common Core Standards: 8.G.2: Understand that a two-dimensional figure is congruent to another if the second can be obtained from the first by a sequence of rotations, reflections, and translations; given two congruent figures, describe a sequence that exhibits the congruence … .

Launch

Your neighbor drew three kites on the grid. She said they were all exactly the same. Do you agree? Explain how you know.

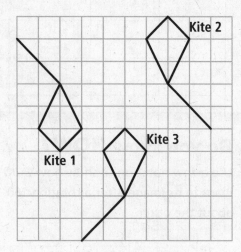

Reflect

How can two shapes be exactly the same but look different?

_____

_____

_____

_____

Close and Check

Focus Question

In what ways can you show that figures are identical?

_____

_____

_____

_____

Do you know HOW?

1. Use arrow notation to show how △ABC maps to its image after a reflection across the x-axis followed by a reflection across the y-axis.

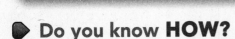
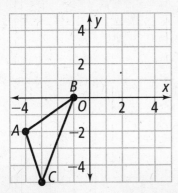

A(⬜) → A'(⬜)

B(⬜) → B'(⬜)

C(⬜) → C'(⬜)

2. What are the vertices of △DEF, the image of △ABC above, after a reflection across the y-axis followed by a 180° rotation clockwise around the origin?

D( )   E( )   F( )

Do you UNDERSTAND?

3. Reasoning Assume △ABC in Problem 1 is rotated 180° about point B. What other transformation(s) could you use to map △ABC to △A'B'C'?

_____

_____

_____

4. Writing Describe a sequence of rigid motions that maps PQRST to P'Q'R'S'T'.

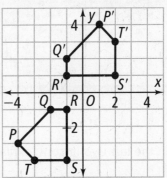

_____

_____

_____

_____

Problem Solving

Common Core Standards: 8.G.2: Understand that a two-dimensional figure is congruent to another if the second can be obtained from the first by a sequence of rotations, reflections, and translations; given two congruent figures, describe a sequence that exhibits the congruence . . . .

Launch

Draw and label three congruent figures. Each figure must be composed of more than one shape. Describe the moves needed to verify that the figures are congruent.

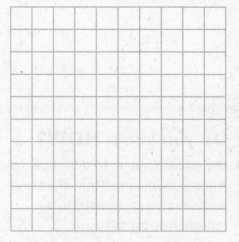

Reflect

Besides in the last two lessons, explain how you have used or could use congruence in your life.

_____

_____

_____

_____

Close and Check

Focus Question

How can you use what you know about transformations and congruence to solve problems?

_____

_____

_____

_____

Do you know HOW?

1. Given figure $ABCDEF \cong LMNPQR$, circle the sequence of rigid motions that maps $ABCDEF$ to $LMNPQR$.

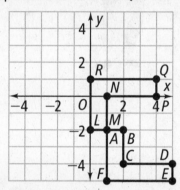

A. Reflection across x-axis, rotation 90° clockwise about point B', translation 1 unit right

B. Rotation 180° counterclockwise about point A', reflection across y-axis, translation 2 units left

C. Reflection across y-axis, rotation 180° clockwise about point A', translation 1 unit right

D. Rotation 90° counterclockwise about point C', translation 2 units left, reflection across $y = 1$

Do you UNDERSTAND?

2. Reasoning Given $\triangle PQR \cong \triangle STU$, explain how to find a possible coordinate for point T.

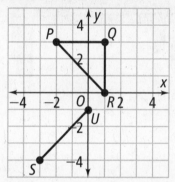

_____

_____

_____

3. Writing Explain why there are two possible coordinates for point T.

_____

_____

_____

_____

_____

Dilations

Common Core State Standards: 8.G.3: Describe the effect of dilations, translations, rotations, and reflections on two-dimensional figures using coordinates.

Launch

A modern art painter used an inch-grid canvas for a figure painting.

Did the artist paint the figure to scale? Explain.

Reflect

Why did the artist have to scale the painting?

_____

_____

_____

_____

Close and Check

Focus Question

What effect does an enlargement have on a figure? What effect does a reduction have on a figure?

_____

_____

_____

_____

Do you know HOW?

1. Find the scale factor for the given dilation and tell whether the image is an enlargement or a reduction.

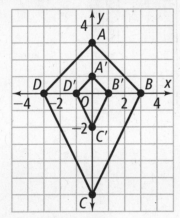

2. Parallelogram *QRST* has vertices at *Q*(−3, 1), *R*(2, 1), *S*(0, −2), and *T*(−5, −2). Find the coordinate of *Q'* after a dilation with the center at the origin and scale factor 5.

Do you UNDERSTAND?

3. Writing △*XYZ* has vertex *Y*(0, 0). The center of the dilation is at the origin. Describe the location of *Y'* after a dilation with scale factor $\frac{1}{5}$. Explain.

_____

_____

_____

_____

_____

4. Error Analysis A classmate creates dilation *A"B"C"D"* for Exercise 1 with the origin at the center with scale factor 4. She says the coordinates are *A"*(0, 5), *B"*(5, 0), *C"*(0, −6), and *D"*(−5, 0). Explain her error.

_____

_____

_____

_____

_____

Similar Figures

Common Core State Standards: 8.G.3: Describe the effect of dilations . . . . **8.G.4:** Understand that a . . . figure is similar to another if the second can be obtained from the first by a sequence of . . . dilations; given two similar . . . figures, describe a sequence that exhibits the similarity between them.

Launch

The artist continues to paint the figure in different sizes on the inch-grid canvas. She stops and says, "One of these shapes clearly doesn't belong. I'd better start over."

Which shape does not belong? Explain your reasoning.

Reflect

Do shapes have to be the same size to belong together? Explain.

_____

_____

_____

_____

Close and Check

Focus Question

How can you show that figures are similar?

_____

_____

_____

_____

▶ Do you know HOW?

1. Given trapezoid *QRST*, draw trapezoid *WXYZ* ~ *QRST* after a 90° clockwise rotation about the origin followed by a dilation with center (0, 0) and scale factor $\frac{1}{2}$.

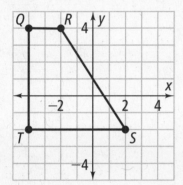

2. What would be the coordinates of *JKLM* ~ *QRST* after a reflection across the *y*-axis and a dilation with the center at the origin and scale factor 2?

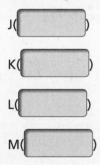

J( )

K( )

L( )

M( )

▶ Do you UNDERSTAND?

3. Writing How would the figure in Exercise 1 change if trapezoid *QRST* were translated up 1 unit and right 3 units followed by a dilation with center (0, 0) and scale factor 1? Explain.

_____

_____

_____

_____

4. Compare and Contrast How are a pair of congruent figures and a pair of similar figures alike? How are they different?

_____

_____

_____

_____

_____

Relating Similar Triangles and Slope

Common Core State Standards: 8.G.3: Describe the effect of dilations ... . **8.G.4:** Understand that a ... figure is similar to another ... . **8.EE.6:** Use similar triangles to explain why the slope *m* is the same between any two distinct points on a non-vertical line in the coordinate plane ... .

Launch

A museum displays the artist's right triangle series. The series features right triangles painted in proportion on each painting. One painting is a fake. Which is it? Explain how you know.

Painting A   **Painting B**   **Painting C**

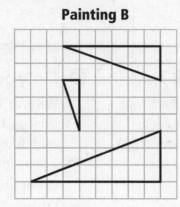 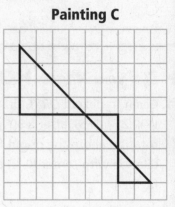

Reflect

For which painting was it easiest to find equivalent ratios? Explain.

_____

_____

_____

_____

Close and Check

▶ **Focus Question**

How are similar triangles and slope related?

_____

_____

_____

▶ **Do you know HOW?**

1. Consider the image △XYZ after a dilation with center (0, 0) and scale factor 2. What is the ratio of the rise to the run of the image triangle?

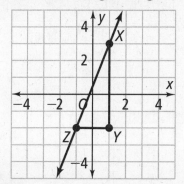

2. What is the slope of the image of △XYZ in Exercise 1 after a 180° rotation about point Y and a dilation with center (0, 0) and scale factor $\frac{1}{3}$?

▶ **Do you UNDERSTAND?**

3. Writing Explain how you can use slope to check the accuracy of a dilation.

_____

_____

_____

_____

4. Error Analysis Your friend uses the slope triangle below to write the equation of the line: $y = \frac{1}{3}x + 3$. Explain his error and write the correct equation.

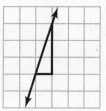

_____

_____

_____

_____

Problem Solving

Common Core State Standards: 8.G.3: Describe the effect of dilations ... . **8.G.4:** Understand that a ... figure is similar to another if the second can be obtained from the first by a sequence of ... dilations; given two similar ... figures, describe a sequence that exhibits the similarity between them.

Launch

Use the criteria to draw your own modern art figure painting on the grid. Give your painting a name.

Explain how your work of art meets the criteria.

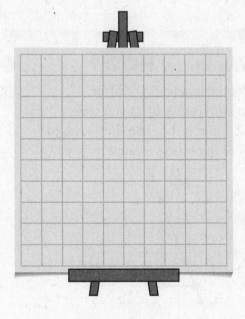

Criteria

- Three of the figures are similar.
- Has at least one dilation.
- Has at least one translation, rotation, or reflection.

Title of Painting:

Reflect

How did you choose your painting's name?

_____

_____

_____

_____

Close and Check

Focus Question

How can you use what you know about transformations and similarity to solve problems?

_____

_____

_____

_____

▶ Do you know **HOW?**

1. Given $\triangle ABC \sim \triangle EFG$, circle the possible coordinate pair(s) for point G after a dilation only.

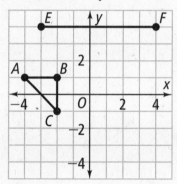

A. $(4, -3)$ B. $(-3, -3)$

C. $(-3, 11)$ D. $(4, 11)$

2. A landscaper makes a scale drawing of a triangular flowerbed. The side lengths of the drawing 3 cm, 4 cm, and 5 cm. If the scale is 2 cm = 7 m, what are the dimensions of the actual flowerbed?

3 cm = [   ]

4 cm = [   ]

5 cm = [   ]

▶ Do you **UNDERSTAND?**

3. Reasoning Explain how scale drawings and indirect measurements are similar. Give an example of how one is used in real life.

_____

_____

_____

_____

4. Error Analysis A friend is 5.5 ft tall and her shadow is 8 ft long. The shadow of a building is 160 ft long. Explain her error in calculating the height of the building. What is the actual height?

$$\frac{5.5}{160} = \frac{8}{x}; \ x = 27 \text{ ft}$$

_____

_____

_____

_____

Angles, Lines, and Transversals

Common Core State Standards: 8.G.5: Use informal arguments to establish facts about the angle sum and exterior angle of triangles, about the angles created when parallel lines are cut by a transversal, and the angle-angle criterion for similarity of triangles ... .

Launch

Which angles have equal measures? Justify your reasoning.

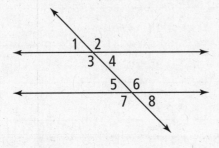

Reflect

Where have you seen angles like these in the real world? Explain.

_____

_____

_____

_____

Close and Check

Focus Question

If a line intersects two parallel lines, what are the relationships between the angles formed by the lines?

_____

_____

_____

_____

Do you know **HOW?**

Use the diagram to complete Exercises 1–4.

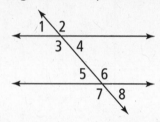

1. Name the pairs of corresponding angles.

2. Name the pairs of alternate interior angles.

3. If $m\angle 4 = 50°$, what is $m\angle 8$?

4. If $m\angle 6 = 130°$, what is $m\angle 3$?

Do you **UNDERSTAND?**

5. Reasoning How many different angle measures are there in the diagram? Explain.

_____

_____

_____

_____

_____

6. Vocabulary What must be true about two lines cut by a transversal if corresponding angles are congruent and alternate interior angles are congruent? Explain.

_____

_____

_____

_____

_____

_____

Reasoning and Parallel Lines

Common Core State Standards: 8.G.5: Use informal arguments to establish facts about the angle sum and exterior angle of triangles, about the angles created when parallel lines are cut by a transversal, and the angle-angle criterion for similarity of triangles ... .

Launch

Decide whether $\overline{AB}$ and $\overline{CD}$ are parallel. Justify your reasoning.

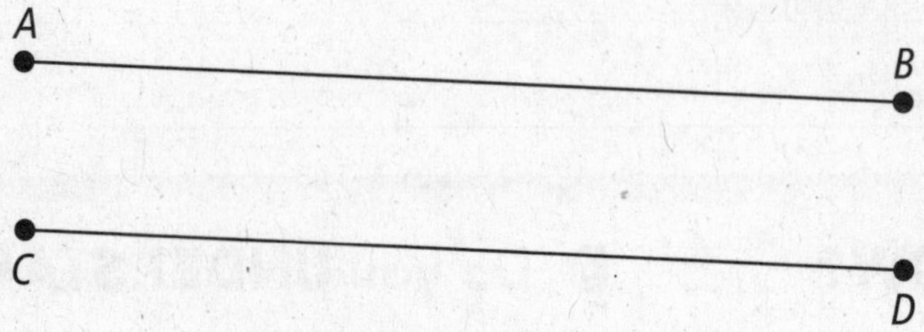

Reflect

What tools or materials did you use to solve the problem? Explain your choice.

_____

_____

_____

_____

Close and Check

Focus Question

How can you use congruent angles to decide whether lines are parallel?

_____

_____

_____

_____

Do you know HOW?

Use the diagram to complete Exercises 1–3.

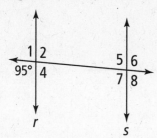

1. For what value of $m\angle 7$ is $r \parallel s$?

2. Write **T** if the statement is true and **F** if the statement is false.

☐ If $m\angle 8 = 95°$, then $r \parallel s$.

☐ If $m\angle 5 = 85°$, then $r \parallel s$.

☐ If $m\angle 6 = 95°$, then $r \parallel s$.

3. If $\angle 7 \cong \angle 2$, then $r \parallel s$ because if

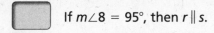 angles are

congruent, then lines are

☐_____ .

Do you UNDERSTAND?

4. Vocabulary Explain how deductive reasoning is used to prove an argument.

_____

_____

_____

_____

_____

_____

5. Reasoning Explain why two lines cannot be assumed to be parallel just because they look parallel.

_____

_____

_____

_____

_____

_____

Interior Angles of Triangles

Common Core State Standards: 8.G.5: Use informal arguments to establish facts about the angle sum and exterior angle of triangles, about the angles created when parallel lines are cut by a transversal, and the angle-angle criterion for similarity of triangles … .

Launch

Which is greater—the measure of a straight angle or the sum of the measures of the angles of a triangle?

Use copies of the triangle to justify your reasoning. You cannot use a protractor.

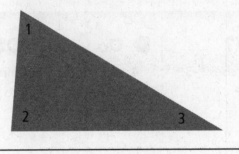

Reflect

Do the angle measures of the triangle you use to compare to the straight angle matter? Explain how you could determine the answer.

_____

_____

_____

_____

Close and Check

Focus Question

How is a straight angle related to the angles of a triangle?

_____

_____

_____

_____

Do you know **HOW?**

Use the diagram to answer Exercises 1–3.

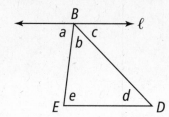

1. Find $m\angle b$, if $m\angle a = 83°$, and $m\angle c = 45°$.

$m\angle b = \boxed{}$

2. Find $m\angle d$, given line $\ell \parallel \overline{ED}$, $m\angle a = 83°$, and $m\angle c = 45°$.

$m\angle d = \boxed{}$

3. Find $m\angle e$, given line $\ell \parallel \overline{ED}$, $m\angle a = 83°$, and $m\angle c = 45°$.

$m\angle e = \boxed{}$

4. What is the value of x when $m\angle b = 10x - 3$, $m\angle d = 5x + 6$, and $m\angle e = 8(x + 2)$?

$x = \boxed{}$

Do you **UNDERSTAND?**

5. Reasoning Use deductive reasoning to justify the solution to Exercise 2.

_____

_____

_____

_____

_____

6. Writing Make a conjecture about the relationship between the two triangles. Justify your reasoning.

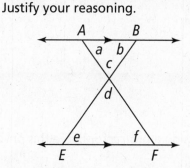

_____

_____

_____

_____

Exterior Angles of Triangles

Common Core State Standards: 8.G.5: Use informal arguments to establish facts about the angle sum and exterior angle of triangles, about the angles created when parallel lines are cut by a transversal, and the angle-angle criterion for similarity of triangles ... .

Launch

State how the sum of the measures of angles 1, 2, and 3 compares to the sum of the measures of angles 4, 5, and 6. You cannot use a protractor. Justify your reasoning.

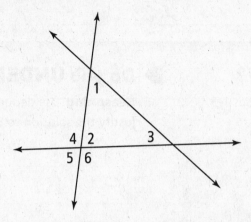

Reflect

Would using a protractor make this problem easier? Explain.

_____

_____

_____

_____

_____

Close and Check

> ## Focus Question
>
> What is the relationship between the exterior and interior angles of a triangle?
>
> _____
>
> _____
>
> _____
>
> _____

▶ Do you know **HOW?**

Use the diagram to solve Exercises 1–4.

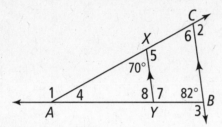

1. Find $m\angle 1$.

2. Find $m\angle 2$.

3. Find $m\angle 3$.

4. Find $m\angle 6$.

5. Given $m\angle 2 = 14x + 9$, and $m\angle 3 = 5x$, what is $m\angle 2$?

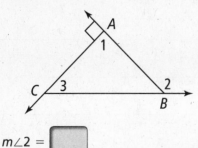

$m\angle 2 = $ [ ]

▶ Do you **UNDERSTAND?**

6. Reasoning How does the sum of the exterior angles of a triangle relate to the sum of the interior angles? Explain.

_____

_____

_____

_____

_____

_____

7. Writing Explain how you found the solution to Exercise 5.

_____

_____

_____

_____

_____

_____

_____

Angle-Angle Triangle Similarity

Common Core State Standards: 8.G.4: Understand that … figure is similar to another if the second can be obtained from the first by … dilations … . **8.G.5:** Use informal arguments to establish facts about … the angle-angle criterion for similarity of triangles … . Also, **8.G.3.**

Launch

Is there a relationship between the triangles? Explain. You can use a protractor, a ruler, and copies of the triangles.

Triangle 1

Triangle 2

Reflect

Could you make another triangle related to either triangle? Explain.

_____

_____

_____

_____

Close and Check

► Focus Question

How can you use angle relationships to decide whether two triangles are similar?

_____

_____

_____

_____

► Do you know **HOW?**

1. Which pair of triangles are similar?

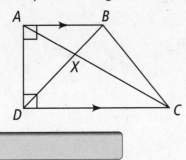

[   ]

2. Use the diagram. Write **T** if the statement is true and **F** if the statement is false.

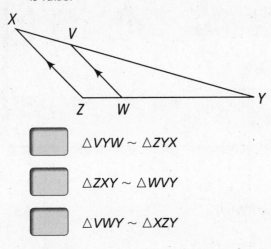

[   ] △VYW ~ △ZYX

[   ] △ZXY ~ △WVY

[   ] △VWY ~ △XZY

► Do you **UNDERSTAND?**

3. Reasoning Given that $BD \parallel AC$, is it possible to conclude that $\triangle ABC \sim \triangle DCB$? Explain.

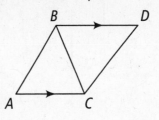

_____

_____

_____

_____

4. Error Analysis Your friend says that if two angles of one triangle are congruent to two angles of another triangle, then the triangles are congruent. Do you agree? Explain.

_____

_____

_____

_____

Problem Solving

Common Core State Standards: 8.G.5: Use informal arguments to establish facts about the angle sum and exterior angle of triangles, about the angles created when parallel lines are cut by a transversal, and the angle-angle criterion for similarity of triangles ... .

Launch

Lines 1 and 2 are parallel horizontal lines. Draw a transversal *p* that passes through point *A* and makes the greatest number of angles with equal angle measure. Justify your reasoning.

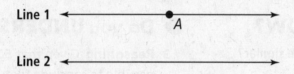

Reflect

How many correct answers does this problem have? Why?

_____

_____

_____

_____

Close and Check

Do you know **HOW?**

Use the diagram to answer Exercises 1 and 2.

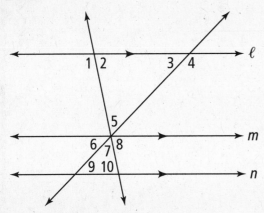

1. Given $\ell \parallel m \parallel n$, and $m\angle 3 = x$, $m\angle 5 = x + 12$, and $m\angle 8 = 2x - 12$, find the angle measures.

$m\angle 2 = \boxed{}$

$m\angle 1 = \boxed{}$

$m\angle 7 = \boxed{}$

$m\angle 4 = \boxed{}$

2. Are the triangles formed by the transversals and parallel lines similar?

Do you **UNDERSTAND?**

3. Reasoning Is it possible to determine the measures of the remaining unlabeled angles in the diagram? Explain your strategy.

_____

_____

_____

_____

_____

_____

_____

4. Error Analysis A classmate says $\angle 6 \cong \angle 8$. Do you agree? Explain.

_____

_____

_____

_____

_____

_____

Reasoning and Proof

Common Core State Standards: 8.G.6: Explain a proof of the Pythagorean Theorem and its converse.

Launch

No one believes the next math genius in line. He claims to know the exact coordinates of the squares that can be formed with the vertices shown, but he can't say why.

Do you believe the next math genius? Justify your reasoning.

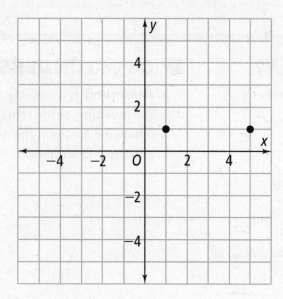

Reflect

Why is it important to justify your reasoning when showing the solution to a problem? Explain.

_____

_____

_____

_____

Close and Check

Focus Question

How can you use deductive reasoning to present a formal mathematical argument?

_____

_____

_____

_____

Do you know HOW?

1. Write the letters of the statements to complete the proof.

Given $5(2y + 4) = 50$, prove $y = 3$.

Statements

A. $10y + 20 = 50$ B. $5(2y + 4) = 50$

C. $y = 3$ D. $10y = 30$

☐ Given

☐ Distributive Property

☐ Subtraction Property of Equality

☐ Division Property of Equality

2. Line x intersects line y. Complete the proof that $m\angle 1 = m\angle 3$.

It is given that ⬚.

$\angle 1 \cong \angle 3$ because $\angle 1$ and $\angle 3$ are

⬚ angles.

$m\angle 1 = m\angle 3$ because ⬚

angles have equal angle measures.

Do you UNDERSTAND?

3. Reasoning Given 1 nickel = 5 pennies and 1 dime = 10 pennies, prove 1 dime = 2 nickels.

_____

_____

_____

_____

_____

_____

_____

4. Writing How can justifying each step of a solution prevent you from making a mistake?

_____

_____

_____

_____

_____

The Pythagorean Theorem

Common Core State Standards: 8.G.6: Explain a proof of the Pythagorean Theorem and its converse.
8.G.7: Apply the Pythagorean Theorem to determine unknown side lengths in right triangles in real-world and mathematical problems in two and three dimensions.

Launch

The squares in Group 1 have a relationship. The squares in Group 2 have the same relationship.

Describe a possible relationship between the squares in each group.

Group 1

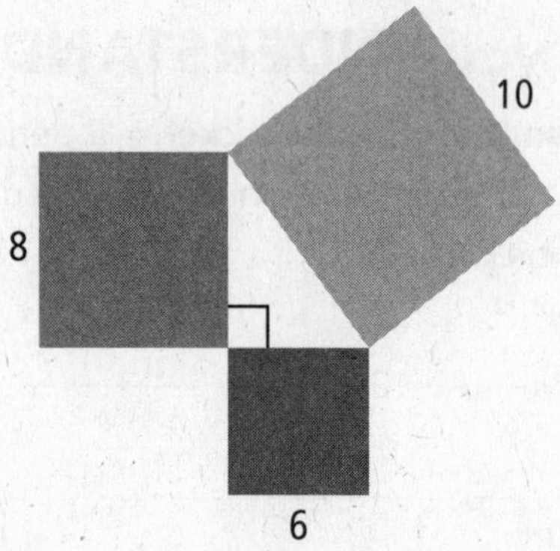

Group 2

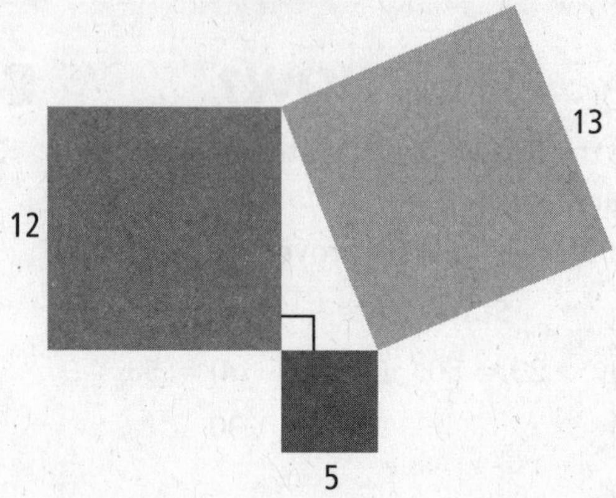

10

8

6

13

12

5

Reflect

Do you think any group of three squares would have this relationship? Explain.

_____

_____

_____

_____

Close and Check

Focus Question

How are the side lengths of a right triangle and the side lengths of squares related?

_____

_____

_____

_____

Do you know HOW?

1. Find the missing length. Round to the nearest tenth.

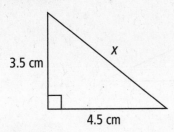

3.5 cm

x

4.5 cm

x = ☐ cm

2. Find the slant height of the pyramid. Round to the nearest whole number.

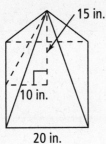

15 in.

10 in.

20 in.

slant height ≈ ☐ in.

Do you UNDERSTAND?

3. Writing If you know the side length of a square, how can you find the length of its diagonal? Explain.

_____

_____

_____

_____

_____

4. Error Analysis Your friend knows that a triangle with side lengths 3, 4, and 5 is a right triangle. She says that the side lengths 5, 6, and 7 must also form a right triangle. Describe her error.

_____

_____

_____

_____

_____

12-3 | Finding Unknown Leg Lengths

Common Core State Standards: 8.G.7: Apply the Pythagorean Theorem to determine unknown side lengths in right triangles in real-world and mathematical problems in two and three dimensions.

Launch

Which three numbers could be the side lengths of the right triangle?
Fill in the values and justify your reasoning.

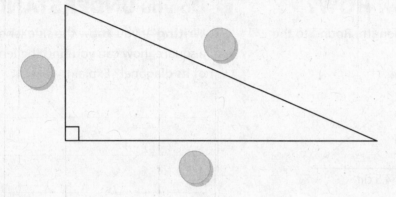

Reflect

Did you try the side lengths or the hypotenuse first when solving the problem? Does it matter? Explain.

_____

_____

_____

Close and Check

Focus Question

When you know the lengths of two sides of a right triangle, how do you find the third?

_____

_____

_____

_____

Do you know **HOW?**

1. Find the height of the sheet of paper. Round to the nearest whole number.

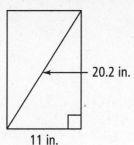

20.2 in.

11 in.

height = [ ] in.

2. Find the height of the square pyramid. Round to the nearest tenth.

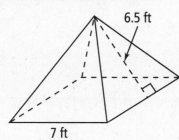

6.5 ft

7 ft

height = [ ] ft

Do you **UNDERSTAND?**

3. Reasoning A square has a diagonal of $\sqrt{50}$. How can you find the side length of the square?

_____

_____

_____

_____

4. Error Analysis Your friend found the height of the square pyramid. Explain her error.

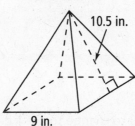

10.5 in.

9 in.

$4.5^2 + 10.5^2 = c^2$

$130.5 = c^2$

$11.4 \approx c$

_____

_____

_____

_____

The Converse of the Pythagorean Theorem

Common Core State Standards: 8.G.6: Explain a proof of the Pythagorean Theorem and its converse.

Launch

The triangle formed by the squares is a right triangle. The squares have side lengths of 6, 8, and 10 units.

Can you use the vertices of squares with these side lengths to make a triangle other than a right triangle? Show and explain your response.

Reflect

What would you need to change to get a different result from your work? Explain.

_____

_____

_____

_____

Close and Check

Focus Question

How can you determine whether a triangle is a right triangle if you do not know its angle measures and do not have measuring tools?

_____

_____

_____

Do you know HOW?

1. Which triangles are right triangles?

I.

16   20

12

II.

10.5   12.5

7.5

III.

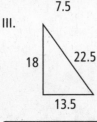

18   22.5

13.5

[   ]

2. Write an **R** in the box to the right of the sides lengths that form a right triangle.

A. 30, 40, 50   [   ]

B. 10, 15, 20   [   ]

C. 18, 24, 30   [   ]

D. 2, 2, 2.8   [   ]

Do you UNDERSTAND?

3. Reasoning Your friend says that since the lengths 3, 4, and 5 form a right triangle, then the lengths 6, 8, and 10 must also form a right triangle. Explain why this works.

_____

_____

_____

_____

4. Writing If you have two 1-inch segments, how can you choose a third segment to make a right triangle? Is there more than one choice you can make? Explain.

_____

_____

_____

_____

_____

Distance in the Coordinate Plane

Common Core State Standards: 8.G.8: Apply the Pythagorean Theorem to find the distance between two points in a coordinate system.

Launch

In which quadrant is the triangle with the greatest perimeter? Justify your reasoning.

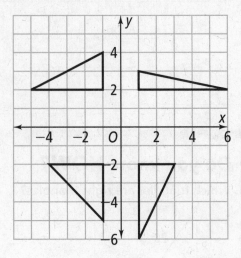

Quadrant II   Quadrant I

Quadrant III   Quadrant IV

Reflect

Which side of the triangle was the key to determining the triangle with the greatest perimeter? Why?

_____

_____

_____

Close and Check

Focus Question

How can you use the Pythagorean Theorem to find the distance between two points?

_____

_____

_____

_____

Do you know HOW?

1. What is the distance between $A(4, 3)$ and $B(-2, 6)$? Round to the nearest tenth.

$c \approx$

2. Classify $\triangle ABC$ by its side lengths. Circle all that apply.

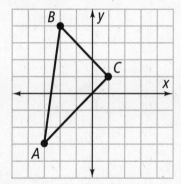

scalene

equilateral

isosceles

right

Do you UNDERSTAND?

3. Compare and Contrast How are finding the distance between two points on a number line and on a coordinate grid alike and different?

_____

_____

_____

_____

_____

4. Writing You walk 3 blocks south and 2 blocks west to the museum. You find the length of the side that forms a right triangle with your path. What actual distance did you find? Is this useful? Explain.

_____

_____

_____

_____

_____

Problem Solving

Common Core State Standards: 8.G.7: Apply the Pythagorean Theorem to determine unknown side lengths in right triangles in real-world and mathematical problems in two and three dimensions.
8.G.8: Apply the Pythagorean Theorem to find the distance between two points in a coordinate system.

Launch

What is the perimeter of a right triangle with an area of 60 in.^{2} and a height of 8 in.?

Provide a picture and justify your response.

Picture	Reasoning

Reflect

Did you draw the picture or do the reasoning first? Explain.

_____

_____

_____

_____

Close and Check

Focus Question

How can you use the Pythagorean Theorem to help you solve real-world and mathematical problems?

_____

_____

_____

▶ Do you know **HOW?**

1. Find the surface area of the square pyramid. Round to the nearest whole number.

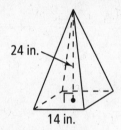

24 in.

14 in.

S.A. ≈ [   ]

2. What is the distance from vertex A to vertex G in the rectangular prism? Round to the nearest tenth.

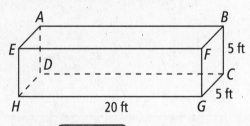

5 ft

5 ft

20 ft

AG = [   ]

▶ Do you **UNDERSTAND?**

3. Error Analysis Your classmate says that the distance from vertex B to vertex H is about 13.4 cm. Explain his error.

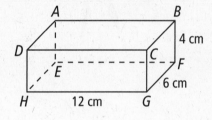

4 cm

6 cm

12 cm

_____

_____

_____

_____

4. Reasoning Can a 39.5-in. golf club fit in a 39 in. by 6 in. by 6 in. packing box? Explain.

_____

_____

_____

_____

Common Core State Standards: 8.G.9: Know the formulas for the volumes of cones, cylinders, and spheres and use them to solve real-world and mathematical problems.

Launch

Your friend invents a new pop-up snake can. She says the height is 5 in. and traces the top of the can on an inch grid.

Draw a label that will cover the whole can except for the top and bottom. Estimate its approximate area. Explain your reasoning.

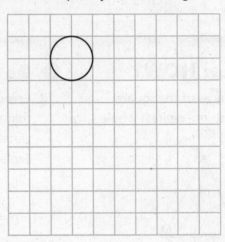

Reflect

What previous mathematical knowledge did you need to solve the problem? Explain.

_____

_____

_____

Close and Check

Focus Question

What types of things can you model with a cylinder? Why might you want to find the surface area of a cylinder?

_____

_____

_____

_____

Do you know **HOW?**

1. Use the net to find the surface area of the cylindrical can to the nearest tenth. Use 3.14 for π.

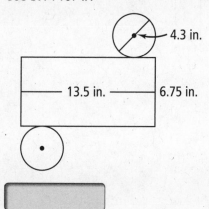

2. Find the surface area of the cylinder to the nearest tenth. Use 3.14 for π.

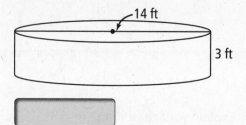

Do you **UNDERSTAND?**

3. Writing Explain how using the calculator key for π rather than 3.14 affects the solution to a surface area problem.

_____

_____

_____

_____

4. Error Analysis Your friend decides that the 2 cylinders have the same surface area. Do you agree? Explain.

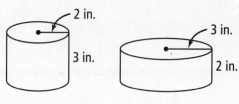

_____

_____

_____

_____

_____

Volumes of Cylinders

Common Core State Standards: 8.G.9: Know the formulas for the volumes of cones, cylinders, and spheres and use them to solve real-world and mathematical problems.

Launch

Your friend claims that 20 in.^{3} of stuffed snake will fit in her new can. Her assistant says, "She better use the box."

Will the can work? Why did the assistant say she should use the box? Explain.

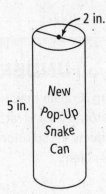
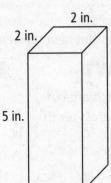

Reflect

How much snake do you think the can would hold? Explain your reasoning.

_____

_____

_____

_____

Close and Check

Why might you want to find the volume of a cylinder?

_____

_____

_____

_____

Do you know HOW?

1. Find the volume. Leave the answer in terms of π.

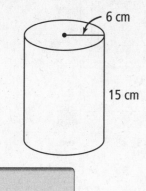

6 cm

15 cm

Do you UNDERSTAND?

3. Reasoning A pitcher holds 1,614.7 in.^{3} of liquid. Each can of punch is 15 in. tall with a diameter of 8 in. How many full cans will the pitcher hold? Explain.

_____

_____

_____

_____

_____

2. The volume of a can of tuna is 562.76 cm^3. Find the radius of the can to the nearest tenth. Use 3.14 for π.

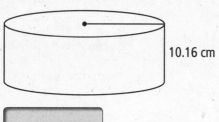

10.16 cm

4. Error Analysis A large can of beans has twice the radius and height of a small can of beans. Your friend says that the large can has twice the volume of the small can. Is he correct? Explain.

_____

_____

_____

_____

_____

_____

Surface Areas of Cones

Common Core State Standards: 8.G.9. Know the formulas for the volumes of cones, cylinders, and spheres and use them to solve real-world and mathematical problems.

Launch

Your friend follows with a plan for a cone-shaped party hat. She says it is 5 in. tall and traces the bottom on the inch grid.

Draw the hat and estimate its surface area. Explain your reasoning.

 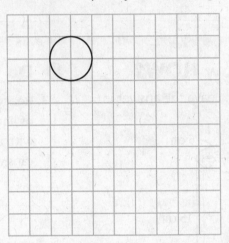

Reflect

Do you think drawing a net of a cone will give you a precise area? Explain.

_____

_____

_____

Close and Check

Focus Question

What types of things can you model with a cone? Why might you want to find the surface area of a cone?

_____

_____

_____

_____

Do you know HOW?

1. Use the net to find the surface area of the cone to the nearest square meter. Use 3.14 for π.

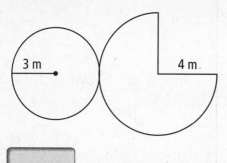

3 m   4 m

[ ]

2. Spiced pecans are sold in cone-shaped containers that include a circular lid. Find the surface area of the container to the nearest square inch. Use 3.14 for π.

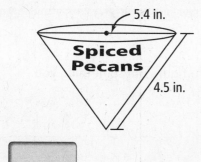

5.4 in.

Spiced Pecans

4.5 in.

[ ]

Do you UNDERSTAND?

3. Compare and Contrast Explain the difference between the height of a cone and the slant height of a cone. How do the measures compare?

_____

_____

_____

_____

_____

_____

_____

4. Reasoning Explain the differences between the surface areas of a cylinder and a cone with the same diameter.

_____

_____

_____

_____

_____

Volumes of Cones

Common Core State Standards: 8.G.9. Know the formulas for the volumes of cones, cylinders, and spheres and use them to solve real-world and mathematical problems.

Launch

Look for a pattern in the volumes of the cylinder and cone pairs in terms of π. Then find the volume of the fourth cone in terms of π. Explain your reasoning.

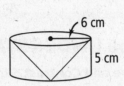

6 cm

5 cm

Cone volume: $60\pi\text{cm}^3$

Cylinder volume:

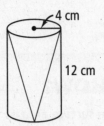

4 cm

12 cm

Cone volume: $64\pi\text{cm}^3$

Cylinder volume:

3 cm

8 cm

Cone volume: $24\pi\text{cm}^3$

Cylinder volume:

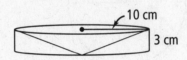

10 cm

3 cm

Cone volume:

Cylinder volume:

Reflect

Describe another situation where you can use a pattern to figure out something you don't know.

_____

_____

_____

_____

Close and Check

Focus Question

Why might you want to find the volume of a cone?

_____

_____

_____

_____

Do you know **HOW?**

1. Number the cones from 1 to 3 in order from least to greatest volume.

5 cm
5 cm

9 cm
3 cm

2 cm
7 cm

2. Find the volume of the funnel to the nearest cubic centimeter. Use 3.14 for π.

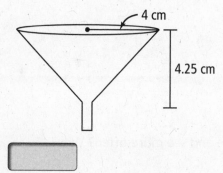
4 cm
4.25 cm

Do you **UNDERSTAND?**

3. Reasoning A juice company repackages individual juice cans in cone-shaped containers with the same volume. The can is 3 in. tall with a diameter of 2 in. What could be the dimensions of the cone container? Explain.

_____

_____

_____

_____

4. Writing A baker pours sugar into a cylindrical jar using the funnel from Exercise 2. If the jar holds 850 cm³, about how many times will he have to fill the funnel before the jar is full? Explain.

_____

_____

_____

_____

Surface Areas of Spheres

Common Core State Standards: 8.G.9. Know the formulas for the volumes of cones, cylinders, and spheres and use them to solve real-world and mathematical problems.

Launch

Which two-dimensional world map, Map #1 or Map #2, would you use to more accurately calculate the surface area of Earth? Explain your reasoning.

  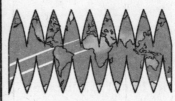

Map #1   **Map #2**

Reflect

Which type of two-dimensional world map do you use and see more often? Why?

_____

_____

_____

_____

Close and Check

Focus Question

What types of things can you model with a sphere? Why might you want to find the surface area of a sphere?

_____

_____

_____

_____

Do you know HOW?

1. Find the surface area of the sphere to the nearest tenth of a square centimeter. Use 3.14 for π.

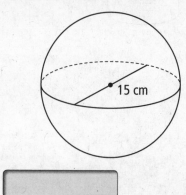
15 cm

[_____]

2. The circumference of a giant beach ball is 383.08 cm. Find the surface area of the beach ball to the nearest tenth of a centimeter. Use 3.14 for π.

[_____]

3. The surface area of a sphere is 651 ft^2. Find the radius of the sphere to the nearest tenth of a square foot. Use 3.14 for π.

[_____]

Do you UNDERSTAND?

4. **Writing** Explain how to use the circumference to find the surface area of a sphere.

_____

_____

_____

_____

_____

5. **Error Analysis** A classmate says it is impossible to find an exact solution for the surface area of a sphere because π is an irrational number. Do you agree? Explain.

_____

_____

_____

_____

_____

Volumes of Spheres

Common Core State Standards: 8.G.9. Know the formulas for the volumes of cones, cylinders, and spheres and use them to solve real-world and mathematical problems.

Launch

Your friend claims that 40 in.³ of party confetti will fit in her new party globe. Her assistant says, "She better use the cylinder."

Will the party globe work? Why did the assistant say she should use the cylinder? Explain.

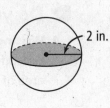

2 in.

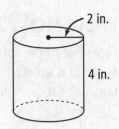

2 in.

4 in.

Reflect

If you had to identify the height and width of a sphere with a radius of 2 inches what would it be?

_____

_____

_____

Close and Check

Focus Question

Why might you want to find the volume of a sphere?

_____

_____

_____

_____

Do you know HOW?

1. To the nearest cubic inch, how much space is there inside the ball for the hamster? Use 3.14 for π.

10 in.

2. A gazing ball in the center of a garden has a volume of 904.3 cm³. To the nearest centimeter, find the diameter of the gazing ball.

3. To the nearest tenth of a cubic foot, find the volume of a 9 ft diameter inflatable ball.

Do you UNDERSTAND?

4. Writing The height and diameter of a cylinder is equal to the diameter of a sphere. Explain the relationship between the volume of the sphere and the volume of the cylinder.

_____

_____

_____

_____

5. Reasoning A ball of twine has a diameter of 3.4 m. More twine is added until the diameter is 12 m. A classmate subtracts the diameters and uses the result to find the change in volume of the sphere. Is he correct? Explain.

_____

_____

_____

_____

_____

_____

Problem Solving

Common Core State Standards: 8.G.9. Know the formulas for the volumes of cones, cylinders, and spheres and use them to solve real-world and mathematical problems.

Launch

The cylinder, cone, and sphere all have the same radius and height (or diameter). Describe how the volumes compare given these dimensions. State the volumes in terms of π.

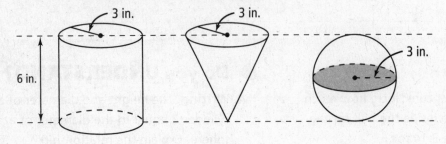

Reflect

How could you use what you know about the relationships between the volumes of the shapes to make solving problems easier? Explain.

_____

_____

_____

_____

Close and Check

Focus Question

How can you apply what you know about surface areas and volumes of cylinders, cones, and spheres to solve problems?

_____

_____

_____

Do you know **HOW?**

1. A greenhouse is built in the shape of half of a sphere. To the nearest tenth of a cubic foot, find the volume of the greenhouse. Use 3.14 for π.

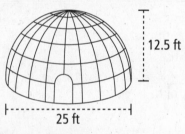

12.5 ft

25 ft

[ ]

2. Find the surface area of the serving dish to the nearest tenth of a square inch. Use 3.14 for π.

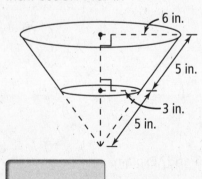

6 in.

5 in.

3 in.

5 in.

[ ]

Do you **UNDERSTAND?**

3. Writing Explain how to find the total volume of the silo.

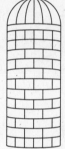

_____

_____

_____

_____

_____

_____

4. Reasoning You want the container with the largest volume. If the height and diameter of each container are equal, should you choose a sphere, cylinder, or cone? Explain.

_____

_____

_____

_____

_____

Interpreting a Scatter Plot

Common Core State Standards: 8.SP.1: Construct and interpret scatter plots for bivariate measurement data to investigate patterns of association between two quantities ....

Launch

Your very precise friend says there's nothing to be learned about the book data because the points don't line up with any exact page or width coordinates. Do you agree? If not, state something you know about at least two of the five books.

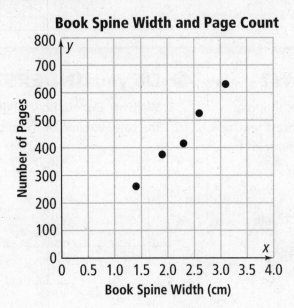

Book Spine Width and Page Count

Reflect

Why don't the book dots hit any intersecting lines on the grid? Explain.

_____

_____

_____

Close and Check

Focus Question

A scatter plot is a graph that shows how two sets of data are related. How are scatter plots better than words or tables for making sense out of real-world data?

_____

_____

_____

_____

Do you know HOW?

Use the scatter plot to answer Exercises 1 and 2.

Practicing Sports

1. What does point (13, 2.5) represent?

2. Write **T** if the statement is true and **F** if the statement is false.

☐ Everyone in the group practices at least half an hour.

☐ Six children practice more than 2 hours each day.

Do you UNDERSTAND?

3. Writing What information could you find more quickly in a scatter plot than in a table? Explain.

_____

_____

_____

_____

4. Error Analysis A classmate says the scatter plot shows that 11 children practice for 2 hours. Do you agree? Explain.

_____

_____

_____

_____

_____

_____

Constructing a Scatter Plot

Common Core State Standards: 8.SP.1: Construct and interpret scatter plots for bivariate measurement data to investigate patterns of association between two quantities ... .

Launch

Conduct your own study of spine widths and page counts. Graph the results for five books. Show your data in another way so you know your scatter plot is correct.

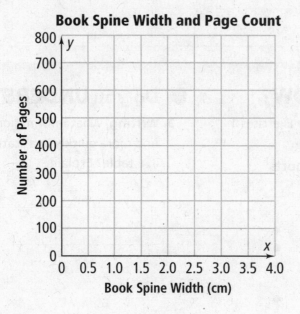

Book Spine Width and Page Count

Reflect

Do you think the scatter plot or your other method displays the data in a better way? Explain.

_____

_____

_____

Close and Check

Focus Question

What characteristics of a data set should you consider in making a scatter plot?

_____

_____

_____

Do you know HOW?

1. The table shows the relationship between hours of sleep each night and the average GPA in your friend's class. Make a scatter plot to represent the data.

The Effect of Sleep on Grades						
Sleep (h)	6	6.5	7	7.5	8	8.5	9
GPA	2.8	3	3.5	3.5	3.7	3.8	3.6

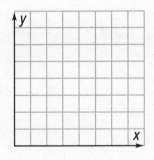

Do you UNDERSTAND?

2. Reasoning You collect data on the height of a group of plants and the amount of sunlight they get daily. Which set of data would you use for the *x*-values and which would you use for the *y*-values? Explain.

_____

_____

_____

_____

3. Writing Explain how to determine the scales for the horizontal and vertical axes of a scatter plot.

_____

_____

_____

_____

Investigating Patterns – Clustering and Outliers

Common Core State Standards: 8.SP.1: ... Describe patterns such as clustering, outliers, positive or negative association, linear association, and nonlinear association.

Launch

The scatter plot shows the spine widths and the page counts of 10 books. Which two books stand out from the rest? What makes them unique?

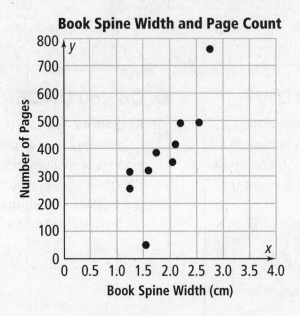

Book Spine Width and Page Count

Reflect

How would the problem be different if the data were in a table not a scatter plot? Explain.

_____

_____

_____

Close and Check

Focus Question

Which features of a scatter plot can best help you to understand the relationship between two data sets?

_____

_____

_____

_____

Do you know **HOW?**

1. Circle the true statement(s) about the scatter plot.

Restaurant Business

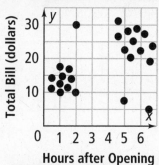

A. Point (2, 30) is an outlier.

B. Most customers spend about the same amount of money.

C. There are two outliers.

D. There are two clusters.

2. What are the coordinates of the outlier(s) in the scatter plot?

Do you **UNDERSTAND?**

3. **Writing** Explain the meanings of the clusters and outliers in the scatter plot in Exercise 1.

_____

_____

_____

_____

_____

_____

4. **Reasoning** Explain how the information in the scatter plot might be useful to the restaurant owner.

_____

_____

_____

_____

_____

_____

Investigating Patterns – Association

Common Core State Standards: 8.SP.1: … Describe patterns such as clustering, outliers, positive or negative association, linear association, and nonlinear association.

Launch

Place 16 coins of several different values in a bag. Remove some coins without looking. Graph the results and put the coins back. Repeat five more times. Tell if you see a relationship between the number of coins you remove and the value of the coins.

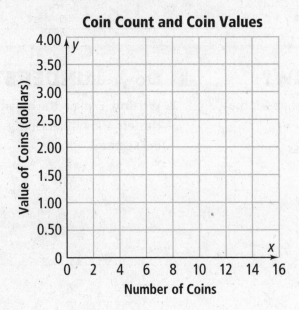

Coin Count and Coin Values

Reflect

Compare your results with those of a friend. Do you have similar results? What could account for the differences?

_____

_____

_____

_____

_____

Close and Check

> **Focus Question**
> Scatter plots show how two sets of data are related. What types of associations result from making a scatter plot? How will you know them when you see them?
>
> _____
>
> _____
>
> _____
>
> _____
>
> _____

Do you know HOW?

1. Determine whether the data in the scatter plot have a *positive*, *negative*, or *no* association.

Educational Trends

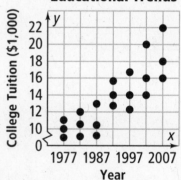

[_____] association

For Exercises 2 and 3, write *positive*, *negative*, or *no* association to describe the relationship between the data.

2. The number of items purchased and the total amount of the bill

[_____] association

3. The height of a person and how many pets he/she owns

[_____] association

Do you UNDERSTAND?

4. Writing Explain your answer to Exercise 1. Why do you think the data have the association you chose?

_____

_____

5. Error Analysis Your friend says that the scatter plot has a cluster and no association. Do you agree? Explain

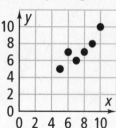

_____

_____

_____

Linear Models – Fitting a Straight Line

Common Core State Standards: 8.SP.2: ... For scatter plots that suggest a linear association, informally fit a straight line, and informally assess the model fit by judging the closeness of the data points to the line.

Launch

Your friend starts drawing lines to connect the results of picking coins from a bag. He says the data show no association between the number of coins and the value of the coins because the lines are so different. Do you agree with your friend? Explain.

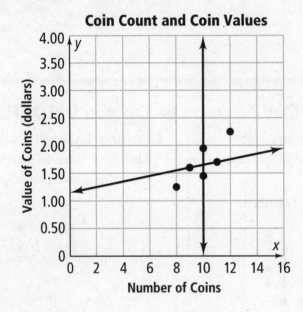

Coin Count and Coin Values

Reflect

How are points on any line related? Explain.

_____

_____

_____

_____

Close and Check

Focus Question

How can a scatter plot have more than one linear model? How do you decide which model to use?

_____

_____

_____

_____

Do you know HOW?

1. Which trend line is the most appropriate for the scatter plot?

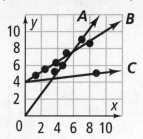

[gray box]

2. Find a trend line and its equation using the scatter plot.

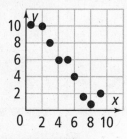

[gray box]

Do you UNDERSTAND?

3. Writing Is it easier to draw the trend line first, and then select two points on the line, or to select two points first, then draw the trend line? Explain.

_____

_____

_____

_____

4. Reasoning Where would be the most accurate placement of a trend line for the scatter plot shown? Explain.

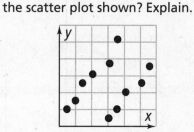

_____

_____

_____

_____

Using the Equation of a Linear Model

Common Core State Standards: 8.SP.3: Use the equation of a linear model to solve problems in the context of bivariate measurement data, interpreting the slope and intercept .... Also, **8.SP.2.**

Launch

Which scatter plot would be most useful and which would be least useful for making a prediction of what sales at week 5 might be?

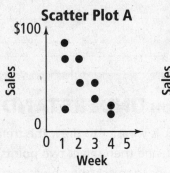
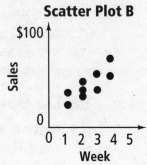
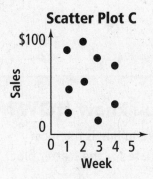

Most Useful:

Least Useful:

Reflect

What was most important for you in the scatter plots for making a prediction?

_____

_____

_____

_____

Close and Check

Focus Question

How can scatter plots help you to make predictions or draw conclusions?

_____

_____

_____

_____

Do you know HOW?

1. Use the scatter plot to write an equation for a trend line.

Gym Membership

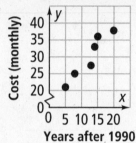

Years after 1990

[ ]

2. Using the linear model from Exercise 1, what would you expect the gym membership to have cost in 1993?

[ ]

3. Using the linear model from Exercise 1, what year would you expect the gym membership to cost $60 per month?

[ ]

Do you UNDERSTAND?

4. Writing Based on the linear model from Exercise 1, is the expected cost of gym membership the same as the actual cost in 2010? Explain.

_____

_____

_____

_____

_____

5. Reasoning Your friend draws a trend line for the scatter plot in Exercise 1 using the points (5, 20) and (20, 37.5). Would you use his points or the points (5, 21) and (15, 36) to draw a trend line? Explain.

_____

_____

_____

_____

_____

Common Core State Standards: 8.SP.2: ... For scatter plots that suggest a linear association, informally fit a straight line, and informally assess the model fit by judging the closeness of the data points to the line.

Launch

Befuddled botanists bemoan the growth of a venomous giant hogweed in their beautiful botanical garden. The biennial plant literally bolts skyward in its Year 2 growing season.

Predict the plant's height at week 12 of Year 2. Justify your reasoning.

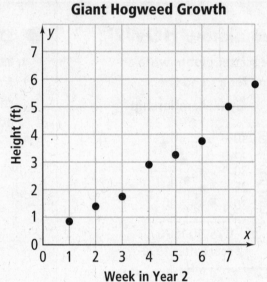

Reflect

What is most critical to making an accurate prediction of the plant's height at Week 12?

_____

_____

_____

_____

Close and Check

Focus Question

Which problems are best solved using scatter plots and their trend lines?

_____

_____

_____

_____

Do you know HOW?

1. Separate the points in the scatter plot into three equal groups. Find the summary point for each group.

Berry Flake Cereal

Group 1: [   ]

Group 2: [   ]

Group 3: [   ]

2. Write an equation for the line through the first and third summary points.

[   ]

3. Write the equation for the median-median trend line for the berry cereal data.

[   ]

Do you UNDERSTAND?

4. Reasoning Line *A* is a trend line including all the data points and Line *B* is a trend line that excludes outliers. How do the outliers effect the position of the line? Explain.

Apartment Rent

_____

_____

_____

_____

_____

_____

Bivariate Categorical Data

Common Core State Standards: 8.SP.4: Understand that patterns of association can also be seen in bivariate categorical data by displaying frequencies and relative frequencies in a two-way table .... .

Launch

Two competing Web-radio rock stations blast listeners with the online surveys shown. Why do you think Station B asked the second question? Explain your reasoning.

Station A

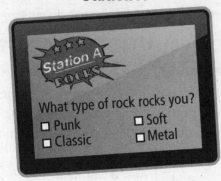

Station B

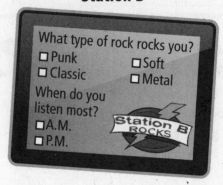

Reflect

Are there benefits to both surveys? If so, what are they?

_____

_____

_____

_____

Close and Check

Focus Question

What does it mean to have bivariate categorical data? What does the data tell you about a population?

_____

_____

_____

Do you know HOW?

1. Indicate whether each variable has values that are *categorical data* or *measurement data*.

Grade Level: [   ]

Weight: [   ]

Song Length: [   ]

2. Circle the survey you can use to collect bivariate categorical data.

Survey 1
What grade are you in?
How long did you spend on homework last night?

Survey 2
What is your favorite subject in school?
What is your favorite sport?

Survey 3
How many siblings do you have?
What is your favorite snack?

Do you UNDERSTAND?

3. Writing You want to see whether there is an association between gender and wearing shoes with laces. Design a survey to collect bivariate categorical data.

_____

_____

_____

_____

_____

4. Vocabulary Identify the variables, the categories, and the groups the data will fall in for your survey.

_____

_____

_____

_____

_____

_____

15-2 / Constructing Two-Way Frequency Tables

Common Core State Standards: 8.SP.4: Understand that patterns of association can also be seen in bivariate categorical data by displaying frequencies … in a two-way table. Construct … a two-way table summarizing data on two categorical variables collected from the same subjects … .

Launch

The tables show the survey results on the type of rock music listeners prefer and the time of day they most often listen.

What do you like about how the tables display the results? How could Station B have made a better table?

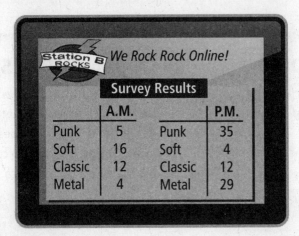

We Rock Rock Online!

Survey Results

	A.M.		P.M.
Punk	5	Punk	35
Soft	16	Soft	4
Classic	12	Classic	12
Metal	4	Metal	29

What I Like:

What Could Be Better:

Reflect

What matters most about how you display survey data?

_____

_____

_____

_____

Close and Check

Focus Question

What is a two-way table? When you construct a two-way frequency table, what does the table show?

_____

_____

_____

_____

Do you know HOW?

1. You ask 80 students whether they own a portable music player. Half of the 50 eighth graders said yes, and 28 seventh graders said yes. Complete the two-way frequency table.

		Music Player?		
		Yes	No	Total
Grade Level	7th			
	8th			
	Total			

2. You ask all 8th graders whether they participate in an after-school activity. Complete the two-way frequency table.

		After-School Activity?		
		Yes	No	Total
Gender	Male		40	
	Female			95
	Total	102		187

Do you UNDERSTAND?

3. **Reasoning** Explain how you found the number of 7th graders who do not have a portable music player in Exercise 1.

_____

_____

_____

_____

4. **Error Analysis** You and a friend take turns interviewing 35 people at the mall. You record that 18 download apps online. Your friend records that 25 own a tablet computer. Can you claim that 18 people download apps onto their tablet computers? Explain.

_____

_____

_____

Interpreting Two-Way Frequency Tables

Common Core State Standards: 8.SP.4: Understand that patterns of association can also be seen in bivariate categorical data by displaying frequencies ... in a two-way table. ... interpret a two-way table summarizing data on two categorical variables collected from the same subjects ... .

Launch

Web-radio rock Station B posts survey results about the type of rock that rocks its male and female listeners.

Describe the two most important things you see in the results. Explain why they are the most important.

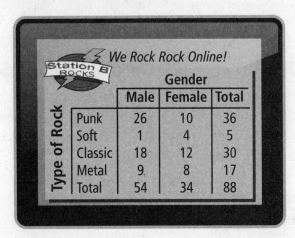

We Rock Rock Online!

Type of Rock	Gender		
	Male	Female	Total
Punk	26	10	36
Soft	1	4	5
Classic	18	12	30
Metal	9	8	17
Total	54	34	88

Two Most Important Things

1.

2.

Why They Are The Most Important

Reflect

Do you like the way the station shows the survey results in this table? Explain.

_____

_____

Close and Check

Focus Question

What can a two-way frequency table tell you about a population?

_____

_____

_____

_____

Do you know HOW?

The table below shows the results of a survey about the subject engineers said was their favorite in middle school.

		Subject		
		Math	Science	Total
Engineer	Electrical	85	90	175
	Chemical	80	91	171
	Mechanical	89	81	170
	Total	254	262	516

1. How many chemical engineers chose science?

☐

2. How many engineers chose math?

☐

3. Based on the table above, write **T** or **F** to classify each statement as true or false.

☐ More engineers chose science than chose math.

☐ More chemical engineers were surveyed than electrical or mechanical engineers.

Do you UNDERSTAND?

4. Reasoning You survey friends about the type of party they enjoy most. What type of party would you plan for them? Explain.

		Gender		
		Male	Female	Total
Party Type?	Bowling	6	2	8
	Skating	3	11	14
	Dancing	1	3	4
	Total	10	16	26

_____

_____

_____

5. Reasoning Your friend uses the data and plans a bowling party. Explain why he may have chosen bowling.

_____

_____

_____

Constructing Two-Way Relative Frequency Tables

Common Core State Standards: 8.SP.4: Understand that patterns of association can also be seen in bivariate categorical data by displaying … relative frequencies in a two-way table. Construct … a two-way table summarizing data on two categorical variables collected from the same subjects … .

Launch

Web-radio Station J surveys DJs about the type of jazz to jazz on Saturday. The station manager wants to use percents instead of raw numbers in the table.

She thinks she can use 50% or 100% for the male total. Explain how both percents could be correct.

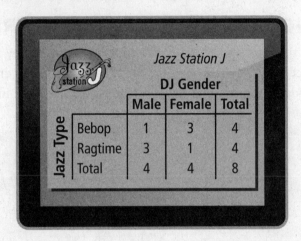

Reflect

Does the choice of 50% or 100% for the male total affect the percents used for bebop and ragtime for males? Explain.

_____

_____

_____

_____

Close and Check

Focus Question

What is a two-way relative frequency table? How is a two-way relative frequency table different from a two-way frequency table?

_____

_____

_____

_____

Do you know HOW?

A recent poll asked whether customers liked a restaurant's new lunch menu. Use the results shown below for Exercise 1.

Frequency Table

		New Menu?		
		Yes	No	Total
Gender	Male	13	15	28
	Female	18	25	43
	Total	31	40	71

1. Complete the corresponding relative frequency table with respect to the total population.

Total Relative Frequency Table

		New Menu?		
		Yes	No	Total
Gender	Male			
	Female			
	Total			

Do you UNDERSTAND?

2. Vocabulary You create a frequency table based on survey results about club membership in a middle school. Explain what the shaded box would represent for each type of relative frequency table.

		Club		
		Drama	Debate	Total
Grade Level	6th			
	7th			
	8th			
	Total			

a. Row Relative Frequency Table

_____

_____

b. Column Relative Frequency Table

_____

_____

_____

Interpreting Two-Way Relative Frequency Tables

Common Core State Standards: 8.SP.4: … Interpret a two-way table summarizing data on two categorical variables collected from the same subjects. Use relative frequencies calculated for rows or columns to describe possible association between the two variables.

Launch

Web-radio Station J plans an online music store. It surveys equal numbers of its two main listener groups—teenagers and adults—about their preferred format for buying jazz.

Provide two pieces of advice to Station J about setting up its online store based on the data.

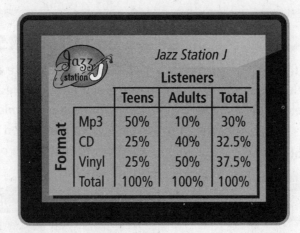

Jazz Station J

Format	Listeners		
	Teens	**Adults**	**Total**
Mp3	50%	10%	30%
CD	25%	40%	32.5%
Vinyl	25%	50%	37.5%
Total	100%	100%	100%

Two Pieces of Advice

1.

2.

Reflect

Could a classmate have different pieces of advice about the same data? Explain.

_____

_____

_____

_____

Close and Check

Focus Question

What can a two-way relative frequency table tell you about a population?

_____

_____

_____

_____

Do you know HOW?

1. What percent of those who studied for 2–4 hours passed the test?

Total Relative Frequency Table

		Hours Studied		
		1–2	2–4	Total
Test Results	Passed	16%	42%	58%
	Failed	30%	12%	42%
	Total	46%	54%	100%

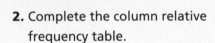

2. Complete the column relative frequency table.

Column Total Relative Frequency Table

		Handedness		
		Left	Right	Total
Hair Color	Blonde	25%	21.2%	22.2%
	Brunette		36.4%	
	Redhead	12.5%	12.2%	12.2%
	Other	29.2%		30%
	Total	100%	100%	

Do you UNDERSTAND?

3. Writing Describe the association between hours studied and test results, if any.

_____

_____

_____

_____

_____

4. Reasoning According to the table in Exercise 2, is there any evidence that hair color and handedness are related? Explain.

_____

_____

_____

_____

_____

_____

_____

Choosing a Measure of Frequency

Common Core State Standards: 8.SP.4: Understand that patterns of association can also be seen in bivariate categorical data by displaying frequencies and relative frequencies in a two-way table. ... Use relative frequencies ... to describe possible association between the two variables.

Launch

Station J asks salespeople (S) and disc jockeys (DJ) to vote on whether a horn or saxophone on the new logo would better communicate that the station plays jazz.

Show the results in a frequency table or a relative frequency table. Justify your choice of table.

New Logo

Votes for Sax	Votes for Horn
DJ DJ S	DJ S
DJ S DJ	DJ S
DJ DJ	

Frequency Table

		Station Workers		
		Sales	DJs	Total
Logo	Horn			
	Sax			
	Total			

Reflect

What conclusions can you draw from your table?

_____

_____

_____

_____

Close and Check

Focus Question

When might you want to use a two-way frequency table? When might you want to use a two-way relative frequency table?

_____

_____

_____

_____

Do you know **HOW?**

1. Circle the table that will be more helpful in finding whether male or female teenagers are more likely to own a car.

Frequency Table

Survey Results		Car Ownership		
		Yes	No	Total
	Male	49	126	175
	Female	48	102	150
	Total	97	228	325

Row Relative Frequency Table

Survey Results		Car Ownership		
		Yes	No	Total
	Male	28%	72%	100%
	Female	32%	68%	100%
	Total	29.8%	70.2%	100%

2. You want to compare the number of male students in marching band to the number of female students in marching band. Would a frequency table or relative frequency table be more useful?

_____

Do you **UNDERSTAND?**

3. Writing Explain how you decided the answer to Exercise 2.

_____

_____

_____

_____

_____

4. Error Analysis A classmate wants to know if age influences movie attendance. He decides to analyze the data using a frequency table. Do you agree with his choice? Explain.

_____

_____

_____

_____

_____

_____

15-7 Problem Solving

Common Core State Standards: 8.SP.4: ... Construct and interpret a two-way table summarizing data on two categorical variables collected from the same subjects. Use relative frequencies calculated for rows or columns to describe possible association between the two variables.

Launch

The table shows survey results from big city and small town residents about their favorite type of Web-radio music.

What's the most important conclusion about city size and music choice you can make? What's the evidence supporting it? Explain.

		Listener Location		
		Big City	Small Town	Total
Type of Music	**Rock**	27%	20%	23.5%
	R & B	25%	20%	22.5%
	Country	23%	55%	39%
	Jazz	25%	5%	15%
	Total	100%	100%	100%

Most Important Conclusion:

Evidence:

Reflect

Could someone else come up with a different most important conclusion? Explain.

_____

_____

_____

Close and Check

Focus Question

How can you determine which two-way table will be most useful in answering a certain question?

_____

_____

_____

_____

Do you know HOW?

1. A city planner conducts a survey of adult residents on whether they have a library card and whether they have an interest in buying an eReader. Complete the tables.

Frequency Table

		Interest in eReader		
		Yes	No	Total
Library Card	Yes		75	
	No	45		
	Total	130		325

Total Relative Frequency Table

		Interest in eReader		
		Yes	No	Total
Library Card	Yes	26%		
	No			51%
	Total	40%		100%

Do you UNDERSTAND?

2. **Reasoning** Is there evidence that having a library card makes you more or less interested in buying an eReader? Explain.

_____

_____

_____

3. **Reasoning** What could explain the interest or lack of interest in buying eReaders among library-card holders?

_____

_____

Formulas

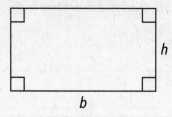

$$P = 2b + 2h$$
$$A = bh$$

Rectangle

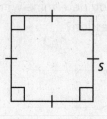

$$P = 4s$$
$$A = s^2$$

Square

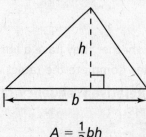

$$A = \frac{1}{2}bh$$

Triangle

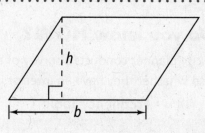

$$A = bh$$

Parallelogram

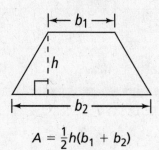

$$A = \frac{1}{2}h(b_1 + b_2)$$

Trapezoid

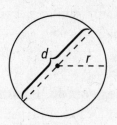

$$C = 2\pi r \text{ or } C = \pi d$$
$$A = \pi r^2$$

Circle

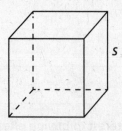

$$\text{S.A.} = 6s^2$$
$$V = s^3$$

Cube

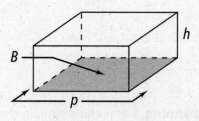

$$V = Bh$$
$$\text{L.A.} = ph$$
$$\text{S.A.} = \text{L.A.} + 2B$$

Rectangular Prism

Formulas

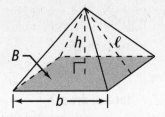

$V = \frac{1}{3}Bh$

L.A. $= 2b\ell$

S.A. $=$ L.A. $+ B$

Square Pyramid

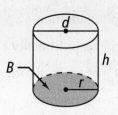

$V = Bh$

L.A. $= 2\pi rh$

S.A. $=$ L.A. $+ 2B$

Cylinder

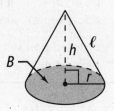

$V = \frac{1}{3}Bh$

L.A. $= \pi r\ell$

S.A. $=$ L.A. $+ B$

Cone

$V = \frac{4}{3}\pi r^3$

S.A. $= 4\pi r^2$

Sphere

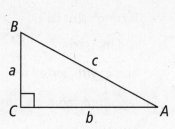

$a^2 + b^2 = c^2$

Pythagorean Theorem

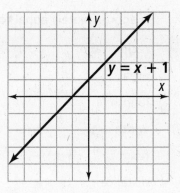

$y = x + 1$

$y = mx + b$, where
$m =$ slope and
$b = y$-intercept

Equation of Line

Math Symbols

+	plus (addition)		r	radius
−	minus (subtraction)		S.A.	surface area
×, ·	times (multiplication)		B	area of base
$\div, \overline{)}, \frac{a}{b}$	divide (division)		L.A.	lateral area
=	is equal to		ℓ	slant height
<	is less than		V	volume
>	is greater than		a^n	nth power of a
≤	is less than or equal to		$\sqrt{x}$	nonnegative square root of x
≥	is greater than or equal to		π	pi, an irrational number approximately equal to 3.14
≠	is not equal to			
( )	parentheses for grouping		(a, b)	ordered pair with x-coordinate a and y-coordinate b
[ ]	brackets for grouping			
$-a$	opposite of a		$\overline{AB}$	segment AB
. . .	and so on		A'	image of A, A prime
°	degrees		$\triangle ABC$	triangle with vertices A, B, and C
$|a|$	absolute value of a			
$\overset{?}{=}, \overset{?}{<}, \overset{?}{>}$	Is the statement true?		→	arrow notation
≈	is approximately equal to		$a : b, \frac{a}{b}$	ratio of a to b
$\frac{b}{a}$	reciprocal of $\frac{a}{b}$		≅	is congruent to
A	area		~	is similar to
ℓ	length		$\angle A$	angle with vertex A
w	width		AB	length of segment $\overline{AB}$
h	height		$\overrightarrow{AB}$	ray AB
d	distance		$\angle ABC$	angle formed by $\overrightarrow{BA}$ and $\overrightarrow{BC}$
r	rate		$m\angle ABC$	measure of angle ABC
t	time		⊥	is perpendicular to
P	perimeter		$\overleftrightarrow{AB}$	line AB
b	base length		‖	is parallel to
C	circumference		%	percent
d	diameter		P (event)	probability of an event

Measures

Customary	Metric
Length	**Length**
1 foot (ft) = 12 inches (in.) 1 yard (yd) = 36 in. 1 yd = 3 ft 1 mile (mi) = 5,280 ft 1 mi = 1,760 yd	1 centimeter (cm) = 10 millimeters (mm) 1 meter (m) = 100 cm 1 kilometer (km) = 1,000 m 1 mm = 0.001 m
Area	**Area**
1 square foot (ft^2) = 144 square inches (in.^{2}) 1 square yard (yd^2) = 9 ft^2 1 square mile (mi^2) = 640 acres	1 square centimeter (cm^2) = 100 square millimeters (mm^2) 1 square meter (m^2) = 10,000 cm^2
Volume	**Volume**
1 cubic foot (ft^3) = 1,728 cubic inches (in.^{3}) 1 cubic yard (yd^3) = 27 ft^3	1 cubic centimeter (cm^3) = 1,000 cubic millimeters (mm^3) 1 cubic meter (m^3) = 1,000,000 cm^3
Mass	**Mass**
1 pound (lb) = 16 ounces (oz) 1 ton (t) = 2,000 lb	1 gram (g) = 1,000 milligrams (mg) 1 kilogram (kg) = 1,000 g
Capacity	**Capacity**
1 cup (c) = 8 fluid ounces (fl oz) 1 pint (pt) = 2 c 1 quart (qt) = 2 pt 1 gallon (gal) = 4 qt	1 liter (L) = 1,000 milliliters (mL) 1000 liters = 1 kiloliter (kL)

Customary Units and Metric Units	
Length	1 in. = 2.54 cm 1 mi ≈ 1.61 km 1 ft ≈ 0.3 m
Capacity	1 qt ≈ 0.94 L
Weight and Mass	1 oz ≈ 28.3 g 1 lb ≈ 0.45 kg

Properties

Unless otherwise stated, the variables *a, b, c, m,* and *n* used in these
properties can be replaced with any number represented on a number line.

Identity Properties
Addition $n + 0 = n$ and $0 + n = n$

Multiplication $n \cdot 1 = n$ and $1 \cdot n = n$

Commutative Properties
Addition $a + b = b + a$

Multiplication $a \cdot b = b \cdot a$

Associative Properties
Addition $(a + b) + c = a + (b + c)$

Multiplication $(a \cdot b) \cdot c = a \cdot (b \cdot c)$

Inverse Properties
Addition

$a + (-a) = 0$ and $-a + a = 0$

Multiplication

$a \cdot \frac{1}{a} = 1$ and $\frac{1}{a} \cdot a = 1, (a \neq 0)$

Distributive Properties

$a(b + c) = ab + ac \quad (b + c)a = ba + ca$

$a(b - c) = ab - ac \quad (b - c)a = ba - ca$

Properties of Equality
Addition   If $a = b$,

              then $a + c = b + c$.

Subtraction   If $a = b$,

              then $a - c = b - c$.

Multiplication If $a = b$,

              then $a \cdot c = b \cdot c$.

Division   If $a = b$, and $c \neq 0$,

              then $\frac{a}{c} = \frac{b}{c}$.

Substitution   If $a = b$, then b can

              replace a in any

              expression.

Zero Property
$a \cdot 0 = 0$ and $0 \cdot a = 0$.

Properties of Inequality
Addition   If $a > b$,

              then $a + c > b + c$.

              If $a < b$,

              then $a + c < b + c$.

Subtraction   If $a > b$,

              then $a - c > b - c$.

              If $a < b$,

              then $a - c < b - c$.

Multiplication

If $a > b$ and $c > 0$, then $ac > bc$.

If $a < b$ and $c > 0$, then $ac < bc$.

If $a > b$ and $c < 0$, then $ac < bc$.

If $a < b$ and $c < 0$, then $ac > bc$.

Division

If $a > b$ and $c > 0$, then $\frac{a}{c} > \frac{b}{c}$.

If $a < b$ and $c > 0$, then $\frac{a}{c} < \frac{b}{c}$.

If $a > b$ and $c < 0$, then $\frac{a}{c} < \frac{b}{c}$.

If $a < b$ and $c < 0$, then $\frac{a}{c} > \frac{b}{c}$.

Properties of Exponents
For any nonzero number n and any
integers m and n:

Zero Exponent $a^0 = 1$

Negative Exponent $a^{-n} = \frac{1}{a^n}$

Product of Powers $a^m \cdot a^n = a^{m+n}$

Power of a Product $(ab)^n = a^n b^n$

Quotient of Powers $\frac{a^m}{a^n} = a^{m-n}$

Power of a Quotient $\left(\frac{a}{b}\right)^n = \frac{a^n}{b^n}$

Power of a Power $(a^m)^n = a^{mn}$